LONGMAN LITERATU

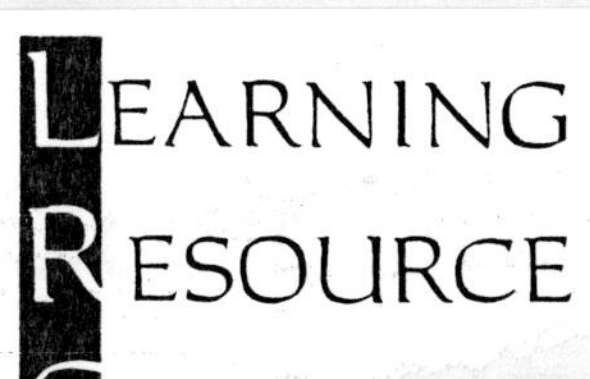

...am Shakespeare

Editor: Iain Veitch

Longman Literature
Series editor: Roy Blatchford

Plays

Alan Ayckbourn **_Absurd Person Singular_** 0 582 06020 6
Ad de Bont **_Mirad, A Boy from Bosnia_** 0 582 24949 X
Oliver Goldsmith **_She Stoops to Conquer_** 0 582 25397 7
Henrik Ibsen **_Three plays: The Wild Duck, Ghosts and A Doll's House_** 0 582 24948 1
Ben Jonson **_Volpone_** 0 582 25408 6
Christopher Marlowe **_Doctor Faustus_** 0 582 25409 4
Arthur Miller **_An Enemy of the People_** 0 582 09717 7
Terence Rattigan **_The Winslow Boy_** 0 582 06019 2
Jack Rosenthal **_Wide-Eyed and Legless_** 0 582 24950 3
Willy Russell **_Educating Rita_** 0 582 06013 3
Shirley Valentine 0 582 08173 4
Peter Shaffer **_Equus_** 0 582 09712 6
The Royal Hunt of the Sun 0 582 06014 1
Bernard Shaw **_Arms and the Man_** 0 582 07785 0
The Devil's Disciple 0 582 25410 8
Pygmalion 0 582 06015 X
Saint Joan 0 582 07786 9
R B Sheridan **_The Rivals_** and **_The School for Scandal_** 0 582 25396 9
J Webster **_The Duchess of Malfi_** 0 582 28731 6
Oscar Wilde **_The Importance of Being Earnest_** 0 582 07784 2

Longman Literature Shakespeare
Series editor: Roy Blatchford

Antony and Cleopatra 0 582 28727 8 (paper)
As You Like It 0 582 23661 4 (paper)
Coriolanus 0 582 28726 X
Hamlet 0 582 09720 7 (paper)
Henry IV Part I 0 582 23660 6 (paper)
Henry V 0 582 22584 1 (paper)
Julius Caesar 0 582 08828 3 (paper)
0 582 24589 3 (cased)
King Lear 0 582 09718 5 (paper)
Macbeth 0 582 08827 5 (paper)
0 582 24592 3 (cased)
The Merchant of Venice 0 582 08835 6 (paper)
0 582 24593 1 (cased)
A Midsummer Night's Dream 0 582 08833 X (paper)
0 582 24590 7 (cased)
Othello 0 582 09719 3 (paper)
Richard III 0 582 23663 0 (paper)
Romeo and Juliet 0 582 08836 4 (paper)
0 582 24591 5 (cased)
The Tempest 0 582 22583 3 (paper)
Twelfth Night 0 582 08834 8 (paper)
The Winter's Tale 0 582 28728 6

Other titles in the Longman Literature series are listed on page 431.

Contents

Introduction

Shakespeare's life and times

Shakespeare was born into a time of change. Important discoveries about the world were changing people's whole way of life, their thoughts and their beliefs. The fact that we know very little of Shakespeare's particular life story does not mean that we cannot step into his world.

What do we know about Shakespeare?

Imagine for a minute you are Shakespeare, born in 1564, the son of a businessman who is making his way in Stratford-upon-Avon. When you are thirteen, Francis Drake sets off on a dangerous sea voyage around the world, to prove that it is round, not flat, and to bring back riches. The trades people who pass in and out of your town bring with them stories of other countries, each with their own unique culture and language. You learn in school of ancient heroic myths taught through Latin and Greek, and often, to bring these stories alive, travelling theatres pass through the town acting, singing, performing, and bringing with them tales of London. But, at the age of fourteen your own world shifts a little under your feet; your father has got into serious debt, you find yourself having to grow up rather fast.

This is an unremarkable life so far – the death of your sisters is not an uncommon occurrence at this time, and when you marry at eighteen, your bride already pregnant at the ceremony, you are not the first to begin your marriage this way. After a daughter, your wife gives birth to twins, a girl and a boy, one of whom dies when he is eleven. But before this, for some reason only you know, perhaps to do with some poaching you are involved in or because your marriage to a woman eight years older than you is having difficulties, you travel to London. There you eventually join the theatre, first as an actor and then as a writer. You write for the theatres in the inn yards, then for Queen Elizabeth in court, and, when she dies, for King James I. As well as this you write for the large theatres which are being built in London: the Rose, the Globe, Blackfriars and the Swan. You die a rich man.

What did Shakespeare find in London?

When Shakespeare first travelled to London he found a city full of all that was best and worst in this new era of discovery. There was trade in expensive and fashionable items, a bubbling street life with street-theatre, pedlars of every sort, sellers of songs and poems. Industry was flourishing in textiles, mining, the manufacture of glass, iron and sugar. The place to be known was the court of Queen Elizabeth. She was unmarried and drew many admirers even in her old age, maintaining a dazzling social world with her at its centre. There were writers and poets, grasping what they could of the new world, building on the literature of other countries, charting the lingering death of medieval life and the chaotic birth of something new.

By contrast, Shakespeare also found poverty, death and disease. The plague, spread by rats, found an easy home in these narrow streets, often spilling over with dirt and sewage: it killed 15,000 people in London in 1592 alone. It was an overcrowded city: the increased demand for wool for trade brought about the enclosure of land in the countryside, and this, coupled with bad harvests, brought the peasants, thrown off their land and made poor, into London to seek wealth.

What was England like in Shakespeare's day?

England was a proud nation. Elizabeth would not tolerate rivals and destroyed her enemies. In 1587 she had Mary Queen of Scots executed for treason, and in 1588 her navy defeated a huge armada of ships from Spain. Both acts were prompted by religion. In maintaining the Protestant Church of England which her father, King Henry VIII, had established, Elizabeth stood out against a strong Catholic Europe. Within the Protestant religion too, there were divisions, producing extreme groups such as the Puritans who believed that much of the Elizabethan social scene was sinful, the theatres being one of their clearest targets for disapproval. Her power was threatened for other reasons too. In 1594 her doctor was executed for attempting to poison her, and in 1601 one of her favourites, the Earl of Essex, led an unsuccessful revolt against her. When Elizabeth died in 1603 and James I succeeded her, he brought a change. He was a Scottish king, and traditionally Scotland and England had had an uneasy relationship. He was interested in witchcraft and he supported the arts, but not in the same way as Elizabeth had. He too met with treason, in the shape of Guy Fawkes and his followers, who in 1605 attempted to blow up the Houses of Parliament. If Shakespeare needed examples of life at its extremes, he had them all round him, and his closeness to the court meant he understood them more than most.

What other changes did Shakespeare see?

Towards the end of Shakespeare's life, in Italy, a man Shakespeare's age invented the telescope and looked at the stars. His radical discoveries caused him to be thrown out of the Catholic Church. For fifteen centuries people had believed in a picture of the universe as held in crystal spheres with order and beauty, and everything centring around the earth. In this belief the sun, moon and stars were the heavens; they ruled human fate, they were distant and magical. Galileo proved this was not so. So, the world was no longer flat and the earth was not the centre of the universe. It must have felt as if nothing was to be trusted any more.

What do Shakespeare's plays show us about Elizabethan life?

Even without history books much of Shakespeare's life can be seen in his plays. They are written by one who knows of the tragedy of sudden death, and illness, and of the splendour of the life of the court in contrast to urban and rural poverty. He knows the ancient myths of the Greeks and Romans, the history of change in his own country, and, perhaps from reading the translations carried by merchants to London, he knows the literature of Spain and Italy.

His plays also contain all the hustle and bustle of normal life at the time. We see the court fool, the aristocracy, royalty, merchants and the servant classes. We hear of bear-baiting, fortune-telling, entertaining, drinking, dancing and singing. As new changes happen they are brought into the plays, in the form of maps, clocks, or the latest fashions. Shakespeare wrote to perform, and his plays were performed to bring financial reward. He studied his audience closely and produced what they wanted. Sometimes, as with the focus on witchcraft in ***Macbeth*** written for King James I, this was the celebration of something which fascinated them; sometimes, as with the character of Shylock in ***The Merchant of Venice***, it was the mockery of something they despised.

What do Shakespeare's plays tell us about life now?

You can read Shakespeare's plays to find out about Elizabethan life, but in them you will also see reflected back at you the unchanging aspects of humanity. It is as if in all that changed around him, Shakespeare looked for the things that would *not* change – like love, power, honour, friendship and loyalty – and put them to the test. In each he found strength and weakness.

We see *love*:

- at first sight
- which is one-sided
- between young lovers

- in old age
- between members of one family
- lost and found again.

We see *power*:

- used and abused
- in those who seek it
- in those who protect it with loyalty
- in the just and merciful rule of wise leaders
- in the hands of unscrupulous tyrants.

We see *honour*:

- in noble men and women
- lost through foolishness
- stolen away through trickery and disloyalty.

We see *friendship*:

- between men and men, women and women, men and women
- between masters and servants
- put to the test of jealousy, grief and misunderstanding.

These are just some examples of how Shakespeare explored in his plays what it was to be human. He lived for fifty-two years and wrote thirty-seven plays, as well as a great number of poems. Just in terms of output this is a remarkable achievement. What is even more remarkable is the way in which he provides a window for his audiences into all that is truly human, and it is this quality that often touches us today.

What are Comedies, Tragedies and Histories?

When Shakespeare died, his players brought together the works he had written, and had them published. Before this some of the plays had only really existed as actors' scripts written for their parts alone. Many plays in Shakespeare's day and before were not written down at all, but spoken, and kept in people's memories from generation to generation. So, making accurate copies of Shakespeare's plays was not easy and there is still much dispute over how close to the original scripts our current editions are. Ever since they were first published people have tried to make sense of them.

Sometimes they are described under three headings: Comedy, Tragedy and History. The dates given on the chart that follows refer to the dates of the first recorded performances or, if this is not known, the date of first publication. They may have been performed earlier but history has left us no record; dating the plays exactly is therefore difficult.

COMEDY	HISTORY	TRAGEDY
	King John (1590)	
	Henry VI, Part I (1592)	
Comedy of Errors (1594)		*Titus Andronicus* (1594)
The Taming of the Shrew (1594)		
Two Gentlemen of Verona (1594)		
The Merry Wives of Windsor (1597)	*Richard II* (1597)	*Romeo and Juliet* (1597)
	Richard III (1597)	
The Merchant of Venice (1598)	*Henry IV, Part II* (1598)	
Love's Labour's Lost (1598)		
As You Like It (1600)	*Henry V* (1600)	

COMEDY	HISTORY	TRAGEDY
A Midsummer Night's Dream (1600) *Much Ado About Nothing* (1600) *Twelfth Night* (1600) *Troilus and Cressida* (1601)	*Henry VI, Part II* (1600) *Henry VI, Part III* (1600)	
		Hamlet (1602)
Measure for Measure (1604) *All's Well That Ends Well* (1604)	*Henry IV, Part I* (1604)	*Othello* (1604)
		Julius Caesar (1605) *Macbeth* (1606) *King Lear* (1606) *Antony and Cleopatra* (1608) *Timon of Athens* (1608) *Coriolanus* (1608)
Pericles (1609) *Cymbeline* (1611) *The Winter's Tale* (1611) *The Tempest* (1612)	*Henry VIII* (1612)	

Comedy = a play which maintains a thread of joy throughout and ends happily for most of its characters.

Tragedy = a play in which characters must struggle with circumstances and in which most meet death and despair.

History = a play focusing on a real event or series of events which actually happened in the past.

These three headings can be misleading. Many of the comedies have great sadness in them, and there is humour in most of the tragedies, some of which at least point to happier events in the future. Some of the tragedies, like ***Hamlet*** and ***Julius Caesar***, make history their starting point.

We do not know exactly when each play was written but from what we know of when they were performed we can see that Shakespeare began by writing poetry, then histories and comedies. He wrote most of his tragedies in the last ten years of his life, and in his final writings wrote stories full of near-tragic problems which, by the end of the plays, he resolved. Sometimes these final plays (***Pericles***, ***Cymbeline***, ***The Winter's Tale*** and ***The Tempest***) are called Comedies, sometimes they are called Romances or simply The Late Plays.

Where were Shakespeare's plays performed?

Plays in Shakespeare's day were performed in several places, not just in specially designed theatres.

Inn Yard Theatres: Players performed in the open courtyard of Elizabethan inns. These were places where people could drink, eat and stay the night. They were popular places to make a break in a journey and to change or rest horses. Some inns built a permanent platform in the yard, and the audience could stand in the yard itself, or under shelter in the galleries which overlooked the yard. The audiences were lively and used to the active entertainment of bear-baiting, cock-fighting, wrestling and juggling. Plays performed here needed to be action-packed and appealing to a wide audience. In

1574 new regulations were made to control performances in response to the number of fights which regularly broke out in the audience.

Private House Theatres: The rich lords of Elizabethan times would pay travelling theatre companies to play in the large rooms of their own private houses for the benefit of their friends. There was no stage and the audience were all seated. Torches and candles were used to create artificial lighting. Costumes played an important part in creating atmosphere but there were no sets.

Public Hall Theatres: Some town councils would allow performances of plays in their grand halls and council buildings. As well as this, ceremonial halls such as the Queen's courts in Whitehall were frequently used in this way, as were halls at Hampton Court, Richmond and Greenwich Palace. For these performances, designed for a larger audience than those given in private houses, scaffolding would be arranged for tiered seating which would surround a central acting area. Audiences were limited to those with a high social standing.

Public Theatres: Unlike public hall theatres, these theatres were built for the purpose of presenting plays. At the end of the sixteenth century there were about 200,000 people living in London, and eleven public theatres showing performances. Of these, about half a dozen were so large that they seated about 2,000 people. The audiences, who were drawn from all sections of society, paid to see performances which began at 2p.m. The audience sat in covered galleries around a circular acting area which was open air. Whilst the theatres stood within the City of London they were subject to its laws. They could not perform during times of worship, and they were closed during outbreaks of the plague. Theatres were often the scenes of fighting and, because of the trouble this caused, in 1596 performances of plays were forbidden within the city boundaries. Thus, people started building theatres outside the city on the south side of the River Thames.

What were the performances like?

To some extent this depended on the play being performed and the audience watching. A play performed before the court of the queen or king would need to be one that did not offend the ruler. Plays performed in the inn yard or the public theatres needed to have a wide appeal and several distractions such as dancing and music to keep the audience's attention.

Wherever they performed, the players had to create the illusion that the whole world could be seen inside their play. They had no sets, except in some cases tapestries which were hung up to show changes in scenery, but they did have bright costumes in which to perform. Scenes of battle or shipwreck were suggested by words rather than special effects, though we do know that they used burning torches, as it was due to a fire caused by one of these that the first Globe Theatre burnt down during a performance in 1613.

Actors joined together in companies, who would perform several different plays, and be sponsored by the nobility. Shakespeare became a key member of the Lord Chamberlain's company which Queen Elizabeth sponsored, and which went on to be called The King's Men when James I became king.

There were no women on the Elizabethan stage. Most female characters would be played by boys whose voices had not yet broken, or if it was an old character, by a man in the company. Actors carried a reputation for being immoral and ungodly people, and were therefore thought unsuitable company for women. The men of Shakespeare's company became famous for playing particular types of characters such as the fool, the lover or the villain. Shakespeare probably created many of his parts with particular actors in mind.

Where can I find out more about Shakespeare?

Shakespeare is perhaps the world's most famous playwright and there is no shortage of books written about him. In your library or bookshop you will find books which look at:

- Shakespeare's life;
- the history of England under the reign of Queen Elizabeth I and James I;
- European history, art and literature of the sixteenth and seventeenth century;
- discoveries made throughout the world during Elizabethan times;
- characters, themes and ideas in Shakespeare's writing.

In Stratford-upon-Avon, you can visit his birthplace, and much of the town consists of buildings which would have stood in Shakespeare's day. In addition to this there are many museums and exhibitions which tell more about Shakespeare's life and work.

Some theatrical companies today, such as the Royal Shakespeare Company, devote themselves to performing Shakespeare's plays in London, Stratford, and on tour around the country. They are always seeking new ways to bring the plays to life. However, perhaps the best way to find out more about Shakespeare is to study his plays by reading and acting them yourself. Shakespeare wrote about what he knew, and the key to discovering how his mind and emotions worked is to look at what he wrote.

Shakespeare's language

Speaking Shakespeare

It is a cold winter's day, the classroom is stuffy and your mind is firmly fixed on the bell which will signal the end of the day. The only thing standing between you and it is your English lesson, in which you have been told that you will be 'reading a Shakespeare text in preparation for your A-level exam'. An immediate picture forms in your head: you, sitting at a desk, bored out of your mind, dreading the moment when you might be asked to read the unintelligible speeches which make up the plays. You silently curse the dramatist who you feel has written so many plays just to make the lives of students miserable.

Sound familiar?

An important mistake by many students is to think that Shakespeare wrote 'books' which he intended to be studied by others. The truth is that he was a professional dramatist who wrote plays to be acted at The Globe Theatre, amongst others. He depended upon the success of his pieces to make a living and so intended them to be as exciting as possible: he might have wanted his audience to learn from them, to see parallels in history with contemporary situations, but his chief concern was that people should leave his theatre feeling entertained, and so wanting to come back for more. The charge of being 'boring' would be a fatal one to him as it would mean a genuine threat to his means of making a living.

Too often, we miss the magic of Shakespeare today not because we are so different from the audiences in his time, or because the material has dated, but because we have to 'study' the plays rather than 'enjoy' them. This means that we approach them expecting to be bored and so rarely give them a real chance. You will be amazed at how much a play can come to life if you not only expect to be entertained by it but also actually get up and act it out. Only by doing this can you truly experience what Shakespeare intended you to when he set about writing.

A problem remains with the language. You are very keen to be involved but just looking at the speeches makes you feel confused, out of your depth, perhaps even a little sick inside. Before giving up, remember that:

- You are looking at a play which is nearly four hundred years old and the English language has changed considerably since then.

Some words, like 'cudgels' and 'curs', have faded out of use altogether and others have changed their meaning. This means that when one is initially looking at a speech, it is useful also to have one eye on the glossary which runs alongside it as this will often help with the more difficult terms.

- Much of ***Coriolanus*** is written in verse, not because that is how people spoke in Elizabethan times but because Shakespeare was creating a work of art, one in which language could be used to greater effect than in everyday speech.
- The language is dense with imagery and rhetorical tricks, which need thinking about.
- Because of the imagery, speakers quite often say a lot in a few words. When you look at the glossary you will be amazed by how much more room a modern 'translation' of the lines takes, and how much is lost in terms of impact by trying to do this.

It is important to speak and hear the lines because only then can you have a full understanding of how a character is responding to a situation, and thus what type of person they are. For instance, in the text we could see:

CORIOLANUS
No!

We will have no idea how this is being said until we look at the context, think about his character and then try out different ways of saying the word to see which sounds best – is he annoyed? Issuing a command? Expressing genuine surprise? Being sarcastic? The list is endless but each variant would show a different facet of the character and only you can decide, by trying them out, which one to use.

You will not be able to do this until you feel more confident as a reader and the best way to achieve this is to practise. If you are working in a group, you will probably be aiming to give some sort of presentation which will involve you either acting a part or giving feedback on a character. Before you begin to work together, and get engrossed, it is worth spending time individually looking at, and practising reading aloud, your speeches. The following tips are to help you be as fluent as possible:

- Pause at the commas, colons and semi-colons.
- Many of the speeches will be in verse. When reading this, pause at the end of sentences (i.e. where there is a full stop) rather than at the end of lines. This will give you a much firmer grasp of meaning.
- Do not pause at the end of lines unless there is some sort of punctuation.
- Think about what the character is saying and the way they are saying it. Try to put emphasis on the words which are intended to have most impact. This will allow you to see the rhythm of the speech and to spot such devices as alliteration.
- Read at a normal pace and in a normal voice: Shakespearean text should not be spoken very sedately or in a falsely posh voice unless you want to come across as a very hammy actor! Think about how someone in that position now would say the lines and give them as much emotional force as you can. After all, an angry person in the seventeenth century would feel the same way as someone today, even if the words they used were different.
- Do not be embarrassed if you make mistakes. Everyone does and these should be part of the fun of trying the text out rather than seen as something to curl up and die about.

Getting started

Before embarking on a reading of the whole text, get used to the feel of the language by simply concentrating upon small extracts from the play. You will no doubt have been told that ***Coriolanus*** is a political play but you will quickly realise that the language used is more akin to verbal abuse than anything we would hear in Parliament today. Indeed, for much of the time characters express their hatred for each other in no uncertain terms and the overall impression one gets in the play is of noise and discord. In order to get in the mood for this, and to feel a little more confident with the language, find a partner and complete the following exercise.

The extracts below are taken from moments of conflict in the play. Stand opposite your partner and take turns firing the insults at each other in a type of verbal duel, giving each as much venom as you can muster. (It may help to imagine your partner is someone you really despise.) The extracts start with one speaker but soon develop into exchanges of insults.

MARCIUS
… What's the matter, you dissentious rogues
That, rubbing the poor itch of your opinion,
Make yourselves scabs?

(Act 1, scene 1, lines 161–3)

MARCIUS
You souls of geese,
That bear the shapes of men, how have you run
From slaves that apes would beat!

(Act 1, scene 4, lines 34–6)

MARCIUS
I'll fight with none but thee, for I do hate thee
Worse than a promise-breaker.

AUFIDIUS
We hate alike:
Not Afric owns a serpent I abhor
More than fame and envy.

(Act 1, scene 8, lines 1–4)

VOLUMNIA
Oh, y'are well met: the hoarded plague o' th' gods
Requite your love!

(Act 4, scene 2, lines 11–12)

SICINIUS

Are you mankind?

VOLUMNIA

Ay, fool; is that a shame? Note but this, fool:

(Act 4, scene 2, lines 16–17)

AUFIDIUS

Name not the god, thou boy of tears!

CORIOLANUS

Ha!

AUFIDIUS

– no more.

CORIOLANUS

Measureless liar, thou hast made my heart
Too great for what contains it. 'Boy'! O slave!

(Act 5, scene 6, lines 100–2)

Prose and blank verse

Every play by Shakespeare is written partly in *prose*, which is set out like ordinary speech, and partly in *verse*, which may or may not rhyme. If it does not rhyme, then it is called *blank verse*. This verse form usually consists of lines of ten syllables, known as *iambic pentameter*. In each line, a stressed syllable is preceded by a syllable which is unstressed, thus giving the speech a rhythm which is similar to the way we speak today. Therefore, when Coriolanus shouts at the mob,

You common cry of curs, whose breath I hate

(Act 3, scene 3, line 122)

he is using the same speech pattern as your parents might use when they shout at you:

'Tidy your room, you dirty little wretch!'

Do not get too worried about this as the verse is seldom this regular. You will find that, just as in everyday speech, as characters become agitated verse patterns become more irregular and this effect is added to by lines being interrupted, or completed, by others. Thus in the following speech in which Coriolanus is lashing out at his soldiers, who have retreated from the enemy, you will see that few of the lines actually obey the rules of the iambic pentameter form, as odd extra syllables are slipped in:

All the contagion of the south light on you,
You shame of Rome! You herd of – Boils and plagues
Plaster you o'er, that you may be abhorr'd
Farther than seen, and one infect another
Against the wind a mile!

(Act 1, scene 4, lines 30–4)

The effect of this disruption is to give the feeling of a man who is furious and thus spitting out his rage. It is a useful speech to practise because it not only has a definite rhythm imposed upon it by the stressed syllables but also demands that you make use of the punctuation fully if it is to be understandable. Thus, it allows you to put into practice all the lessons you have learned so far.

The usual practice in Shakespearean plays is for the common people to speak in prose whilst the nobles speak in verse, mirroring their greater refinement. ***Coriolanus*** does not fit neatly into this pattern because in much of it nobles and plebians mix, often in wildly different circumstances. However, it is useful to chart the times when characters speak in verse because it gives one an important clue as to their feelings and intentions at any given time. Thus, the rioting citizens in the first Act begin by speaking in prose to one of the city's rulers, Menenius, but soon switch to verse. This could be a sign that he has partly placated them or that they are showing him that they are able to use language to flatter as easily as he is.

Similarly, the tribunes, the leaders of the people, speak in prose when they are privately informing them of what they should do, yet use the more persuasive verse form when they are publicly inciting the mob to banish Coriolanus from the city. The fact that they revert at times to speaking in verse when they are alone together is a sign of their pretensions to nobility, a clear indication of their real reason for gaining election as the citizens' representatives in the Senate.

The message is clear: be awake to the ways in which characters use language and you will be able to make profound insights into their characters.

Imagery

One of the things which makes Shakespeare's language difficult to follow is his use of *imagery*, in particular metaphor, simile and personification. The difference between using such figurative language and straightforward terms is that the former allows one to say far more in fewer words. It also allows the audience to place a greater range of interpretations upon what is said. Therefore, when Coriolanus refers to the mob of citizens as 'the many headed Hydra', he is not only referring to the way that it is made up of many people but also to the way that all are of the same opinion and have made themselves monstrous by the rebellion. The value of the image used in the insult can be seen in the way it captures his contempt for them much more effectively than such a long-winded attempt to explain it!

Simile and metaphor

The language of ***Coriolanus*** is much more Spartan than that of Shakespeare's other tragedies but much use is made of simile and metaphor, particularly when the lead character or the citizens are being described.

A *simile* is a comparison of one object to another which makes use of 'like' or 'as', and tends to state the characteristic which the two things are being contrasted in e.g. he is as fat as a barrel. Thus

Coriolanus is described as, 'like a bear', 'like an eagle' and 'like an engine' whilst he tells the people that he holds as much love for them, 'As the dead carcasses of unburied men' (Act 3, scene 3, line 124).

A *metaphor* is a direct comparison between two objects in which one is said to be the other. In this play, much use is made by Shakespeare of images referring to the hero and the mob as animals, with Coriolanus appearing to the people as 'a very dog to the commonalty' and they to him as 'hares', 'geese', 'minnows' and 'multiplying spawn'.

Therefore, an important way to understand what a person is like is to look at, and think about, the figurative language which is used to describe them both by others and by themselves.

The other dominant images in the play concern:

- eating – and food
- disease – and the human body
- acting – and language.

As you read through the text, chart when such images appear and think about who is using them and why.

The glossary: a word of warning

The glossary is there to help you to make sense of the more difficult speeches and to fill in gaps in your vocabulary. An inevitable consequence of explaining someone else's work is to rob it of much of its force so you would be well advised to use the glossary for your first reading but then concentrate upon Shakespeare's language: only then will you appreciate the true skill of the dramatist.

Coriolanus

CHARACTERS
in the play

CAIUS MARCIUS, *afterwards* CAIUS MARCIUS CORIOLANUS

TITUS LARTIUS }
COMINIUS } *Generals against the Volscians*

MENENIUS AGRIPPA, *friend to Coriolanus*

SICINIUS VELUTUS }
JUNIUS BRUTUS } *Tribunes of the People*

YOUNG MARCUIS, *son to Coriolanus*

A ROMAN HERALD

NICANOR, *a Roman*

TULLUS AUFIDIUS, *General of the Volscians*

LIEUTENANT *to Aufidius*

CONSPIRATORS *with Aufidius*

ADRIAN, *a Volscian*

A CITIZEN OF ANTIUM

TWO VOLSCIAN GUARDS

VOLUMNIA, *mother to Coriolanus*

VIRGILIA, *wife to Coriolanus*

VALERIA, *friend to Virgilia*

GENTLEWOMAN *attending on Virgilia*

ROMAN *and* VOLSCIAN SENATORS, PATRICIANS, ÆDILES, LICTORS, SOLDIERS, CITIZENS, MESSENGERS, SERVANTS *to Aufidius, and other* ATTENDANTS

The action takes place in Rome and its neighbourhood; Corioli and its neighbourhood and Antium.

Act 1: summary

Some citizens are preparing to riot about food shortages in Rome. They intend to confront the city's leaders, the senators, who they believe are storing grain for their own use whilst the poor starve. The first citizen denounces Caius Marcius above all as an enemy of the people. Menenius, a city elder, attempts to calm the mob, telling them there is a genuine shortage of grain and attempting to paint the Senate as wise rulers. Marcius arrives with news that the riot on the far side of the city has been ended by the people being granted tribunes to represent their views. A messenger arrives with news that the Volsces, a neighbouring state, are preparing to attack Rome. Marcius is to join the generals, Cominius and Titus Lartius, in the defence of the city. The two new tribunes, Sicinius and Brutus, lament the opportunity the forthcoming war will give him for further honours. In Corioli, Marcius' main rival, Aufidius, a Volscian general, is also preparing for war.

The Roman army soon meet with the Volsces and Marcius sets out to capture Corioli. Initially he is beaten back but leads a counter-attack which results in the city gates closing him in, alone. He soon emerges bloodied but triumphant and sets out to support his general, whilst the Roman soldiers start looting. Marcius finds Cominius in retreat but spurs the men on to a fresh charge. He meets Aufidius and the two fight.

The Romans are left masters of the field. Cominius, recognising Marcius' heroics, offers him one tenth of the spoils but the latter refuses, unwilling to allow himself to be flattered. He accepts instead a new name, Coriolanus, after the town he has taken single-handed. He is hailed as a hero by all.

The defeated Aufidius, cast out of Corioli, swears to be revenged upon Coriolanus at any cost.

The play is unusual in that it opens in the middle of an urban riot. The citizens are on their way to the Capitol, the temple of Jupiter in Rome, to join rioters from all parts of the city.

Act One

Scene one

Rome. A street.

Enter a company of mutinous CITIZENS, *with staves, clubs, and other weapons.*

1 CITIZEN
Before we proceed any further, hear me speak.

ALL
Speak, speak.

1 CITIZEN
You are all resolv'd rather to die than to famish?

ALL
Resolv'd, resolv'd.

1 CITIZEN
First, you know Caius Marcius is chief enemy to the people.

ALL
We know't, we know't.

1 CITIZEN
Let us kill him, and we'll have corn at our own price. Is't a verdict?

ALL
No more talking on't; let it be done. Away, away!

2 CITIZEN
One word, good citizens.

13–16 ***What authority ... humanely*** the first citizen believes that the people are starving whilst those in authority have a glut of food. He says that if they release their excess grain to the people then they will have acted humanely.

16–19 ***The leanness ... abundance*** the famine which afflicts us, causing misery, is the means by which they illustrate their power.

19–20 ***Let us ... rakes*** a play on the dual meaning of each word. Pikes and rakes are agricultural tools but here he also means them to refer to lances and to being 'thin as a rake'.

25 ***a very dog*** pitiless, cruel. This begins the animal imagery used throughout the play.

25–6 ***commonalty*** common people.

1 CITIZEN

We are accounted poor citizens, the patricians good. What authority surfeits on would relieve us; if they would yield us but the superfluity while it were wholesome, we might guess they relieved us humanely; but they think we are too dear. The leanness that afflicts us, the object of our misery, is as an inventory to particularize their abundance; our sufferance is a gain to them. Let us revenge this with our pikes ere we become rakes; for the gods know I speak this in hunger for bread, not in thirst for revenge.

2 CITIZEN

Would you proceed especially against Caius Marcius?

1 CITIZEN

Against him first; he's a very dog to the commonalty.

2 CITIZEN

Consider you what services he has done for his country?

1 CITIZEN

Very well, and could be content to give him good report for't but that he pays himself with being proud.

2 CITIZEN

Nay, but speak not maliciously.

1 CITIZEN

I say unto you, what he hath done famously he did it to that end; though soft-conscienc'd

36–7 ***partly proud*** the citizen accuses Marcius of serving Rome partly to feed his own self-esteem. This accusation will be repeated throughout the play.

37–8 ***which he is . . . virtue*** those who hate Marcius, nevertheless, recognise his indisputable valour. It is important to realise that, for the Romans, this was the highest virtue, and thus something all should strive for. The citizen gets around this by saying that Marcius is as proud as he is valiant.

52 ***bats and clubs*** these refer to cudgels, used in Shakespeare's time by the London Apprentices when rioting. Note that Menenius, unlike the citizens, speaks in verse because he is a noble. From line 112 the citizens will begin to use verse out of respect – a sign that he has partly placated them.

men can be content to say it was for his country, he did it to please his mother and to be partly proud, which he is, even to the altitude of his virtue.

2 CITIZEN

What he cannot help in his nature you account a vice in him. You must in no way say he is covetous.

1 CITIZEN

If I must not, I need not be barren of accusations; he hath faults, with surplus, to tire in repetition. (*Shouts within*) What shouts are these? The other side o' th' city is risen. Why stay we prating here? To th' Capitol!

ALL

Come, come.

1 CITIZEN

Soft! who comes here?

Enter MENENIUS AGRIPPA.

2 CITIZEN

Worthy Menenius Agrippa; one that hath always lov'd the people.

1 CITIZEN

He's one honest enough; would all the rest were so!

MENENIUS

What work's, my countrymen, in hand? Where
go you
With bats and clubs? The matter? Speak, I pray
you.

56–7 ***They say ... breaths*** they say poor beggars have bad breaths – a frequent jibe about the poor in Elizabethan times.

64 ***dearth*** scarcity.

66–9 ***whose course ... impediment*** which will continue to follow a similar route, breaking through ten thousand restraints more powerful than any obstruction you could make.

72–3 ***You are ... attends you*** your reaction to this disaster will bring more down on you.

1 CITIZEN

Our business is not unknown to th' Senate; they have had inkling this fortnight what we intend to do, which now we'll show 'em in deeds. They say poor suitors have strong breaths; they shall know we have strong arms too.

MENENIUS

Why, masters, my good friends, mine honest neighbours,
Will you undo yourselves?

1 CITIZEN

We cannot, sir; we are undone already.

MENENIUS

I tell you, friends, most charitable care
Have the patricians of you. For your wants,
Your suffering in this dearth, you may as well
Strike at the heaven with your staves as lift them
Against the Roman state; whose course will on
The way it takes, cracking ten thousand curbs
Of more strong link asunder than can ever
Appear in your impediment. For the dearth,
The gods, not the patricians, make it, and
Your knees to them, not arms, must help. Alack,
You are transported by calamity
Thither where more attends you; and you slander
The helms o' th' state, who care for you like fathers,
When you curse them as enemies.

1 CITIZEN

Care for us! True, indeed! They ne'er car'd for us

78 ***usury*** money lending, usually at a very high rate of interest.

82 ***wars eat us not*** the first image of devouring/cannibalism, that recurs throughout the play.

89 ***stale't*** i.e. to make it stale by telling it again.

90–1 ***fob off . . . a tale*** a fob was a cheat. The most fitting translation is trivialise through the trickery of a fable the disgrace done to us.

91 ***an't please you*** if it pleases you.

93 ***There was a time . . .*** 'The Fable of the Belly' comes from Shakespeare's major source, Plutarch's ***Lives of Noble Grecians and Romanes***.

yet. Suffer us to famish, and their storehouses cramm'd with grain; make edicts for usury, to support usurers; repeal daily any wholesome act established against the rich, and provide more piercing statutes daily to chain up and restrain the poor. If the wars eat us not up, they will; and there's all the love they bear us.

MENENIUS

Either you must
Confess yourselves wondrous malicious,
Or be accus'd of folly. I shall tell you
A pretty tale. It may be you have heard it;
But, since it serves my purpose, I will venture
To stale't a little more.

1 CITIZEN

Well, I'll hear it, sir; yet you must not think to fob off our disgrace with a tale. But, an't please you, deliver.

MENENIUS

There was a time when all the body's members
Rebell'd against the belly; thus accus'd it:
That only like a gulf it did remain
I' th' midst o' th' body, idle and unactive,
Still cupboarding the viand, never bearing
Like labour with the rest; where th' other instruments
Did see and hear, devise, instruct, walk, feel,
And, mutually participate, did minister
Unto the appetite and affection common
Of the whole body. The belly answer'd –

105–6 ***but even thus … smile*** the lines suggest that Menenius undertakes some action to make the Belly smile.

112 ***kingly crown'd head*** Elizabethans believed that just as the king was God's representative on Earth, Reason (whose seat/source is the head) was the highest of the senses.

113 ***counsellor heart*** the heart was considered by Shakespeare as the seat of understanding.

115 ***muniments*** fortifications – keeping up the image of the body being like a town under siege.

118 ***cormorant*** greedy.

119 ***sink*** cesspool.

1 CITIZEN
Well, sir, what answer made the belly?

MENENIUS
Sir, I shall tell you. With a kind of smile,
Which ne'er came from the lungs, but even
thus –
For look you, I may make the belly smile
As well as speak – it tauntingly replied
To th' discontented members, the mutinous
parts
That envied his receipt; even so most fitly
As you malign our senators for that
They are not such as you.

1 CITIZEN
Your belly's answer – What?
The kingly crowned head, the vigilant eye,
The counsellor heart, the arm our soldier,
Our steed the leg, the tongue our trumpeter,
With other muniments and petty helps
Is this our fabric, if that they –

MENENIUS
What then?
Fore me, this fellow speaks! What then? What
then?

1 CITIZEN
Should by the cormorant belly be restrain'd,
Who is the sink o' th' body –

MENENIUS
Well, what then?

127 ***incorporate friends*** united in one body.

134 ***cranks*** winding corridors.

offices the sense here is minor organs.

1 CITIZEN
The former agents, if they did complain,
What could the belly answer?

MENENIUS
I will tell you;
If you'll bestow a small – of what you have little –
Patience awhile, you'st hear the belly's answer.

1 CITIZEN
Y'are long about it.

MENENIUS
Note me this, good friend:
Your most grave belly was deliberate,
Not rash like his accusers, and thus answered.
'True is it, my incorporate friends,' quoth he
'That I receive the general food at first
Which you do live upon; and fit it is,
Because I am the storehouse and the shop
Of the whole body. But, if you do remember,
I send it through the rivers of your blood,
Even to the court, the heart, to th' seat o' th' brain;
And, through the cranks and offices of man,
The strongest nerves and small inferior veins
From me receive that natural competency
Whereby they live. And though that all at once
You, my good friends' – this says the belly; mark me.

1 CITIZEN
Ay, sir; well, well.

141–3 ***that all . . . the bran*** all from me do receive the best nourishment, whilst I reserve for myself only the bran.

148 ***weal o' th' common*** general welfare of all.

MENENIUS

'Though all at once cannot
See what I do deliver out to each,
Yet I can make my audit up, that all
From me do back receive the flour of all,
And leave me but the bran.' What say you to't?

1 CITIZEN

It was an answer. How apply you this?

MENENIUS

The senators of Rome are this good belly,
And you the mutinous members; for, examine
Their counsels and their cares, digest things
rightly
Touching the weal o' th' common, you shall find
No public benefit which you receive
But it proceeds or comes from them to you,
And no way from yourselves. What do you think,
You, the great toe of this assembly?

1 CITIZEN

I the great toe? Why the great toe?

MENENIUS

For that, being one o' th' lowest, basest, poorest,
Of this most wise rebellion, thou goest foremost.
Thou rascal, that art worst in blood to run,
Lead'st first to win some vantage.
But make you ready your stiff bats and clubs.
Rome and her rats are at the point of battle;
The one side must have bale.

Enter CAIUS MARCIUS.

Hail, noble Marcius!

161 ***dissentious rogues*** revolting rabble.

163 ***scabs*** Marcius compares the people to sores which, when aggravated, become scabs. A double-edged image: the people both make themselves loathsome in appearance by their revolt and also become irritants to the state of Rome. It introduces the motif of disease into the play.

165 ***curs*** dogs.

170 ***coal of fire upon the ice*** here Marcius applies the image of fire to the citizens yet it is one which will be associated with him throughout the play.

171–3 ***Your virtue ... did it*** you show your true nature by honouring a man who has been rightly punished and cursing the judges who did it.

174–6 ***your affections ... evil*** your desires are like a sick man's appetite, which wants for the very things which will make his disease more virulent.

181 ***garland*** your hero. The most valiant soldier in Roman wars was given an oak garland to wear in the victory parade.

MARCIUS

Thanks. What's the matter, you dissentious rogues
That, rubbing the poor itch of your opinion,
Make yourselves scabs?

1 CITIZEN

We have ever your good word.

MARCIUS

He that will give good words to thee will flatter
Beneath abhorring. What would you have, you curs,
That like nor peace nor war? The one affrights you,
The other makes you proud. He that trusts to you,
Where he should find you lions, finds you hares;
Where foxes, geese; you are no surer, no,
Than is the coal of fire upon the ice
Or hailstone in the sun. Your virtue is
To make him worthy whose offence subdues him,
And curse that justice did it. Who deserves greatness
Deserves your hate; and your affections are
A sick man's appetite, who desires most that
Which would increase his evil. He that depends
Upon your favours swims with fins of lead,
And hews down oaks with rushes. Hang ye! Trust ye?
With every minute you do change a mind
And call him noble that was now your hate,
Him vile that was your garland. What's the matter

190–1 ***give out/Conjectural marriages*** speculate about matches.

194 ***lay aside their ruth*** put aside their pity.

197 ***pick my lance*** hurl my spear.

202 ***an-hungry*** Marcius is mocking the citizens' manner of speech with this fake colloquialism.

That in these several places of the city
You cry against the noble Senate, who,
Under the gods, keep you in awe, which else
Would feed on one another? What's their
seeking?

MENENIUS

For corn at their own rates, whereof they say
The city is well stor'd.

MARCIUS

Hang 'em! They say!
They'll sit by th' fire and presume to know
What's done i' th' Capitol, who's like to rise,
Who thrives and who declines; side factions, and
give out
Conjectural marriages, making parties strong,
And feebling such as stand not in their liking
Below their cobbled shoes. They say there's grain
enough!
Would the nobility lay aside their ruth
And let me use my sword, I'd make a quarry
With thousands of these quarter'd slaves, as high
As I could pick my lance.

MENENIUS

Nay, these are almost thoroughly persuaded;
For though abundantly they lack discretion,
Yet are they passing cowardly. But, I beseech you,
What says the other troop?

MARCIUS

They are dissolv'd. Hang 'em!
They said they were an-hungry; sigh'd forth
proverbs –

208–9 ***To break . . . pale*** to give a final blow to the power of the nobility and to make them look weak. (The word 'power' will be used 38 times in the course of the play.)

214 ***and I know not*** these tribunes never appear. The struggle is personalised, and thus intensified, by making it between Marcius and the two tribunes mentioned here.

219 ***fragments*** scraps of uneaten food; scattered parts of a whole.

That hunger broke stone walls, that dogs must eat,
That meat was made for mouths, that the gods sent not
Corn for the rich men only. With these shreds
They vented their complainings; which being answer'd,
And a petition granted them – a strange one,
To break the heart of generosity
And make bold power look pale – they threw their caps
As they would hang them on the horns o' th' moon,
Shouting their emulation.

MENENIUS

What is granted them?

MARCIUS

Five tribunes, to defend their vulgar wisdoms,
Of their own choice. One's Junius Brutus –
Sicinius Velutus, and I know not. 'Sdeath!
The rabble should have first unroof'd the city
Ere so prevail'd with me; it will in time
Win upon power and throw forth greater themes
For insurrection's arguing.

MENENIUS

This is strange.

MARCIUS

Go get you home, you fragments.

Enter a MESSENGER, *hastily.*

222 ***vent*** to excrete; get rid of.

223 ***musty superfluity*** mouldy excess, i.e. the rebellious citizens. The idea of using wars to get rid of excess population is a common one in Shakespeare's plays.

230 ***Were half . . . ears*** even if half the world were at war with the other half.

MESSENGER
Where's Caius Marcius?

MARCIUS
Here. What's the matter?

MESSENGER
The news is, sir, the Volsces are in arms.

MARCIUS
I am glad on't; then we shall ha' means to vent
Our musty superfluity. See, our best elders.

Enter COMINIUS, TITUS LARTIUS, *with other* SENATORS; JUNIUS BRUTUS *and* SICINIUS VELUTUS.

1 SENATOR
Marcius, 'tis true that you have lately told us:
The Volsces are in arms.

MARCIUS
They have a leader,
Tullus Aufidius, that will put you to't.
I sin in envying his nobility;
And were I anything but what I am,
I would wish me only he.

COMINIUS
You have fought together?

MARCIUS
Were half to half the world by th' ears, and he
Upon my party, I'd revolt, to make
Only my wars with him. He is a lion
That I am proud to hunt.

234 ***Attend upon . . . wars*** the sense is not only 'go with' but also 'serve under', a status which will be commented upon by the tribunes later in this scene.

236 ***constant*** i.e. I will keep my word.

1 SENATOR

Then, worthy Marcius,
Attend upon Cominius to these wars.

COMINIUS

It is your former promise.

MARCIUS

Sir, it is;
And I am constant. Titus Lartius, thou
Shalt see me once more strike at Tullus' face.
What, art thou stiff? Stand'st out?

TITUS LARTIUS

No, Caius, Marcius;
I'll lean upon one crutch and fight with t'other
Ere stay behind this business.

MENENIUS

O, true bred!

1 SENATOR

Your company to th' Capitol; where, I know,
Our greatest friends attend us.

TITUS LARTIUS

(*To* COMINIUS) Lead you on.
(*To* MARCIUS) Follow Cominius; we must follow you;
Right worthy you priority.

COMINIUS

Noble Marcius!

1 SENATOR

(*To the* CITIZENS) Hence to your homes; be gone.

247 ***gnaw their garners*** gnaw at their granaries, i.e. to eat the Volscian stores instead of Rome's.

253 ***Being mov'd ... gods*** being angered, he will sneer even at the gods.

255–6 ***He is grown ... valiant*** his valour makes him too proud. The bitterness of the oath shows that the tribunes are well aware of the political danger a successful Marcius would pose.

MARCIUS

Nay, let them follow.
The Volsces have much corn: take these rats thither
To gnaw their garners. Worshipful mutineers,
Your valour puts well forth; pray follow.

CITIZENS *steal away. Exeunt all but* SICINIUS *and* BRUTUS

SICINIUS

Was ever man so proud as is this Marcius?

BRUTUS

He has no equal.

SICINIUS

When we were chosen tribunes for the people –

BRUTUS

Mark'd you his lip and eyes?

SICINIUS

Nay, but his taunts!

BRUTUS

Being mov'd, he will not spare to gird the gods.

SICINIUS

Bemock the modest moon.

BRUTUS

The present wars devour him! He is grown
Too proud to be so valiant.

SICINIUS

Such a nature,
Tickled with good success, disdains the shadow
Which he treads on at noon. But I do wonder

268 ***Opinion*** i) reputation; ii) public opinion.

269 ***demerits*** merits.

His insolence can brook to be commanded
Under Cominius.

BRUTUS

Fame, at the which he aims –
In whom already he is well grac'd – cannot
Better be held nor more attain'd than by
A place below the first; for what miscarries
Shall be the general's fault, though he perform
To th' utmost of a man, and giddy censure
Will then cry out of Marcius 'O, if he
Had borne the business!'

SICINIUS

Besides, if things go well,
Opinion, that so sticks on Marcius, shall!
Of his demerits rob Cominius.

BRUTUS

Come.
Half all Cominius' honours are to Marcius,
Though Marcius earn'd them not; and all his
  faults
To Marcius shall be honours, though indeed
In aught he merit not.

SICINIUS

Let's hence and hear
How the dispatch is made, and in what fashion,
More than his singularity, he goes
Upon this present action.

BRUTUS

Let's along.

Exeunt

6 ***circumvention*** the opportunity to intercept it.

Scene two

Corioli. The Senate House.

Enter TULLUS AUFIDIUS *with* SENATORS *of* CORIOLI.

1 SENATOR
So, your opinion is, Aufidius,
That they of Rome are ent'red in our counsels
And know how we proceed.

AUFIDIUS
Is it not yours?
What ever have been thought on in this state
That could be brought to bodily act ere Rome
Had circumvention? 'Tis not four days gone
Since I heard thence; these are the words – I think
I have the letter here; yes, here it is:
(*Reads*) 'They have press'd a power, but it is not known
Whether for east or west. The dearth is great;
The people mutinous; and it is rumour'd,
Cominius, Marcius, your old enemy,
Who is of Rome worse hated than of you,
And Titius Lartius, a most valiant Roman,
These three lead on this preparation
Whither 'tis bent. Most likely 'tis for you;
Consider of it'.

1 SENATOR
Our army's in the field;
We never yet made doubt but Rome was ready
To answer us.

21–2 ***which in . . . Rome*** which, as soon as they were put into action, became apparent to Rome.

28 ***the remove*** raising of the siege.

AUFIDIUS

Nor did you think it folly
To keep your great pretences veil'd till when
They needs must show themselves; which in the hatching,
It seem'd, appear'd to Rome. By the discovery
We shall be short'ned in our aim, which was
To take in many towns ere almost Rome
Should know we were afoot.

2 SENATOR

Noble Aufidius,
Take your commission; hie you to your bands;
Let us alone to guard Corioli.
If they set down before's, for the remove
Bring up your army; but I think you'll find
Th'have not prepar'd for us.

AUFIDIUS

O, doubt not that!
I speak from certainties. Nay more,
Some parcels of their power are forth already,
And only hitherward. I leave your honours.
If we and Caius Marcius chance to meet,
'Tis sworn between us we shall ever strike
Till one can do no more.

ALL

The gods assist you!

AUFIDIUS

And keep your honours safe!

1 SENATOR

Farewell.

2 ***comfortable sort*** more comfortable manner.

7 ***comeliness*** pleasantness; attractiveness.

2 SENATOR

Farewell.

ALL

Farewell.

Exeunt

Scene three

Rome. MARCIUS*' house.*

Enter VOLUMNIA, *and* VIRGILIA, *mother and wife to* MARCIUS. *They sit down on two low stools and sew.*

VOLUMNIA

I pray you, daughter, sing, or express yourself in a more comfortable sort. If my son were my husband, I should freelier rejoice in that absence wherein he won honour than in the embracements of his bed where he would show most love. When yet he was but tender-bodied, and the only son of my womb; when youth with comeliness pluck'd all gaze his way; when, for a day of kings' entreaties, a mother should not sell him an hour from her beholding; I, considering how honour would become such a person – that it was no better than picture-like to hang by th' wall, if renown made it not stir – was pleas'd to let him seek danger where he was like to find fame. To a cruel war I sent him, from whence he return'd his brows bound with oak. I tell thee, daughter, I sprang not more in joy at first hearing he was a man-child than now in first seeing he had proved himself a man.

27 ***voluptuously*** the literal meaning relates to excessive sensual pleasure. Volumnia is expressing a choice between military service and the more sensual, luxurious civilian life.

36 ***got*** conceived.

40 ***lose his hire*** lose his position; not be paid.

VIRGILIA

But had he died in the business, madam, how then?

VOLUMNIA

Then his good report should have been my son; I therein would have found issue. Hear me profess sincerely: had I a dozen sons, each in my love alike, and none less dear than thine and my good Marcius, I had rather had eleven die nobly for their country than one voluptuously surfeit out of action.

Enter a GENTLEWOMAN.

GENTLEWOMAN

Madam, the Lady Valeria is come to visit you.

VIRGILIA

Beseech you give me leave to retire myself.

VOLUMNIA

Indeed you shall not.
Methinks I hear hither your husband's drum;
See him pluck Aufidius down by th' hair;
As children from a bear, the Volsces shunning
    him.
Methinks I see him stamp thus, and call thus:
'Come on, you cowards! You were got in fear,
Though you were born in Rome'. His bloody
    brow
With his mail'd hand then wiping, forth he goes,
Like to a harvest-man that's task'd to mow
Or all or lose his hire.

43 ***Hecuba*** queen of Troy.

44 ***Hector*** son of Hecuba and champion of Troy.

45–6 ***when it . . . contemning*** the image is of Hector's wound disdaining the sword which has made it.

VIRGILIA

His bloody brow? O Jupiter, no blood!

VOLUMNIA

Away, you fool! It more becomes a man
Than gilt his trophy. The breasts of Hecuba,
When she did suckle Hector, look'd not lovelier
Than Hector's forehead when it spit forth blood
At Grecian sword, contemning. Tell Valeria
We are fit to bid her welcome.

Exit GENTLEWOMAN

VIRGILIA

Heavens bless my lord from fell Aufidius!

VOLUMNIA

He'll beat Aufidius' head below his knee
And tread upon his neck.

Re-enter GENTLEWOMAN, *with* VALERIA *and an* USHER.

VALERIA

My ladies both, good day to you.

VOLUMNIA

Sweet madam!

VIRGILIA

I am glad to see your ladyship.

VALERIA

How do you both? You are manifest housekeepers. What are you sewing here? A fine spot, in good faith. How does your little son?

VIRGILIA

I thank your ladyship; well, good madam.

69 ***mammocked*** tore it into fragments. A recurring image in the play is dismemberment.

72 ***A crack*** a rogue.

74 ***the idle huswife*** i.e. one who spends her time at social gatherings.

VOLUMNIA

He had rather see the swords and hear a drum than look upon his schoolmaster.

VALERIA

O' my word, the father's son! I'll swear 'tis a very pretty boy. O' my troth, I look'd upon him a Wednesday half an hour together; has such a confirm'd countenance! I saw him run after a gilded butterfly; and when he caught it he let it go again, and after it again, and over and over he comes, and up again, catch'd it again; or whether his fall enrag'd him, or how 'twas, he did so set his teeth and tear it. O, I warrant, how he mammock'd it!

VOLUMNIA

One on's father's moods.

VALERIA

Indeed, la, 'tis a noble child.

VIRGILIA

A crack, madam.

VALERIA

Come, lay aside your stitchery; I must have you play the idle huswife with me this afternoon.

VIRGILIA

No, good madam; I will not out of doors.

VALERIA

Not out of doors!

VOLUMNIA

She shall, she shall.

86 ***Penelope*** the wife of Ulysses, considered the ideal wife because, whilst her husband was fighting at Troy, she stayed indoors and wove. Both Valeria and Volumnia scorn this idea.

88 ***cambric*** fine linen.

VIRGILIA

Indeed, no, by your patience; I'll not over the threshold till my lord return from the wars.

VALERIA

Fie, you confine yourself most unreasonably; come, you must go visit the good lady that lies in.

VIRGILIA

I will wish her speedy strength, and visit her with my prayers; but I cannot go thither.

VOLUMNIA

Why, I pray you?

VIRGILIA

'Tis not to save labour, nor that I want love.

VALERIA

You would be another Penelope; yet they say all the yarn she spun in Ulysses' absence did but fill Ithaca full of moths. Come, I would your cambric were sensible as your finger, that you might leave pricking it for pity. Come, you shall go with us.

VIRGILIA

No, good madam, pardon me; indeed I will not forth.

VALERIA

In truth, la, go with me; and I'll tell you excellent news of your husband.

VIRGILIA

O, good madam, there can be none yet.

VALERIA

Verily, I do not jest with you; there came news from him last night.

109 ***disease our better mirth*** spoil the fun we could have without her.

VIRGILIA
Indeed, madam?

VALERIA
In earnest, it's true; I heard a senator speak it. Thus it is: the Volsces have an army forth; against whom Cominius the general is gone, with one part of our Roman power. Your lord and Titus Lartius are set down before their city Corioli; they nothing doubt prevailing, and to make it brief wars. This is true, on mine honour; and so, I pray, go with us.

VIRGILIA
Give me excuse, good madam; I will obey you in everything hereafter.

VOLUMNIA
Let her alone, lady; as she is now, she will but disease our better mirth.

VALERIA
In troth, I think she would. Fare you well, then. Come, good sweet lady. Prithee, Virgilia, turn thy solemness out o' door and go along with us.

VIRGILIA
No, at a word, madam; indeed I must not. I wish you much mirth.

VALERIA
Well then, farewell.

Exeunt

2 ***My horse ... no*** I'll bet my horse against yours they haven't (met).

Scene four

Before Corioli.

Enter MARCIUS, TITUS LARTIUS, *with drum and colours, with* CAPTAINS *and* SOLDIERS. *To them a* MESSENGER.

MARCIUS
Yonder comes news; a wager – they have met.

TITUS LARTIUS
My horse to yours – no.

MARCIUS
'Tis done.

TITUS LARTIUS
Agreed.

MARCIUS
Say, has our general met the enemy?

MESSENGER
They lie in view, but have not spoke as yet.

TITUS LARTIUS
So, the good horse is mine.

MARCIUS
I'll buy him of you.

TITUS LARTIUS
No, I'll nor sell nor give him; lend you him I will
For half a hundred years. Summon the town.

MARCIUS
How far off lie these armies?

MESSENGER
Within this mile and half.

9 ***'larum*** a call to arms.

11 ***smoking swords*** i.e. steaming with the blood of the enemy.

12 ***fielded friends*** friends already in the field, i.e. Cominius.

16–17 ***We'll break ... us up*** we'll break out of the city rather than allow them to imprison us in it.

21 ***cloven army*** i) divided in two (i.e. Marcius and Cominius are fighting on two fronts); ii) dismembered (i.e. by Aufidius).

MARCIUS

Then shall we hear their 'larum, and they ours.
Now, Mars, I prithee, make us quick in work,
That we with smoking swords may march from hence
To help our fielded friends! Come, blow thy blast.

They sound a parley. Enter two SENATORS *with others, on the walls of Corioli.*

Tullus Aufidius, is he within your walls?

1 SENATOR

No, nor a man that fears you less than he:
That's lesser than a little.

Drum afar off.

Hark, our drums
Are bringing forth our youth. We'll break our walls
Rather than they shall pound us up; our gates,
Which yet seem shut, we have but pinn'd with rushes;
They'll open of themselves.

Alarum far off.

Hark you far off!
There is Aufidius. List what work he makes
Amongst your cloven army.

MARCIUS

O, they are at it!

TITUS LARTIUS

Their noise be our instruction. Ladders, ho!

26 ***much beyond our thoughts*** more than it is possible for us to imagine.

30 ***contagion of the south*** Marcius, once more using disease imagery, is alluding to the idea that the warm southern winds brought with them pestilence.

32 ***abhorr'd . . . mile*** detested before you can be seen (on account of your stench) spreading disease even against a prevailing wind. The image is a complex one but its essence is that Marcius is condemning the soldiers' cowardice, once more picturing the common people as a disease which infects the honour of Rome.

36 ***Pluto and hell!*** an oath – Pluto was the Greek god of the underworld.

38 ***agued fear*** trembling fear (as if feverish).

41 ***beat them to their wives*** i) back to civilian life; ii) back into the city of Corioli.

Enter the army of the Volsces.

MARCIUS

They fear us not, but issue forth their city.
Now put your shields before your hearts, and fight
With hearts more proof than shields. Advance, brave Titus.
They do disdain us much beyond our thoughts,
Which makes me sweat with wrath. Come on, my fellows.
He that retires, I'll take him for a Volsce,
And he shall feel mine edge.

Alarum. The Romans are beaten back to their trenches. Re-enter MARCIUS, *cursing.*

MARCIUS

All the contagion of the south light on you,
You shames of Rome! you herd of – Boils and plagues
Plaster you o'er, that you may be abhorr'd
Farther than seen, and one infect another
Against the wind a mile! You souls of geese
That bear the shapes of men, how have you run
From slaves that apes would beat! Pluto and hell!
All hurt behind! Backs red, and faces pale
With flight and agued fear! Mend and charge home,
Or, by the fires of heaven, I'll leave the foe
And make my wars on you. Look to't. Come on;
If you'll stand fast we'll beat them to their wives,
As they us to our trenches. Follow me.

48 ***To th' pot*** to the cooking pot, i.e. he has been cut to pieces.

Another alarum. The Volsces fly, and MARCIUS *follows them to the gates.*

So, now the gates are ope; now prove good
seconds;
'Tis for the followers fortune widens them,
Not for the fliers. Mark me, and do the like.

MARCIUS *enters the gates.*

1 SOLDIER
Fool-hardiness; not I.

2 SOLDIER
Not I.

MARCIUS *is shut in.*

1 SOLDIER
See, they have shut him in.

ALL
To th' pot, I warrant him.

Alarum continues.

Re-enter TITUS LARTIUS.

TITUS LARTIUS
What is become of Marcius?

ALL
Slain, sir, doubtless.

1 SOLDIER
Following the fliers at the very heels,
With them he enters; who, upon the sudden,
Clapp'd to their gates. He is himself alone,
To answer all the city.

56 ***carbuncle*** a jewel. This introduces into the play the idea of Marcius as something precious. Ironically, the word can also be used for a boil.

58 ***Cato's*** this refers to a Roman writer who had written a treatise on military values.

63 ***make remain alike*** stay there like him.

TITUS LARTIUS

O noble fellow!
Who sensibly outdares his senseless sword,
And when it bows stand'st up. Thou art left, Marcius;
A carbuncle entire, as big as thou art,
Were not so rich a jewel. Thou wast a soldier
Even to Cato's wish, not fierce and terrible
Only in strokes; but with thy grim looks and
The thunder-like percussion of thy sounds
Thou mad'st thine enemies shake, as if the world
Were feverous and did tremble.

Re-enter MARCIUS, *bleeding, assaulted by the enemy.*

1 SOLDIER

Look, sir.

TITUS LARTIUS

O, 'tis Marcius!
Let's fetch him off, or make remain alike.

They fight, and all enter the city.

Scene five

Within Corioli. A street.

Enter certain ROMANS, *with spoils.*

1 ROMAN
This will I carry to Rome.

2 ROMAN
And I this.

4–5 ***See here . . . drachma!*** look at these scavengers who value their time in terms of a virtually worthless coin, i.e. will waste their time collecting worthless loot.

6 ***Irons of a doit*** weapons worth virtually nothing.

3 ROMAN

A murrain on't! I took this for silver.

Alarum continues still afar off.

Enter MARCIUS *and* TITUS LARTIUS *with a trumpeter.*

MARCIUS

See here these movers that do prize their hours
At a crack'd drachma! Cushions, leaden spoons,
Irons of a doit, doublets that hangmen would
Bury with those that wore them, these base
slaves,
Ere yet the fight be done, pack up. Down with
them!

Exeunt pillagers

And hark, what noise the general makes! To him!
There is the man of my soul's hate, Aufidius,
Piercing our Romans; then, valiant Titus, take
Convenient numbers to make good the city;
Whilst I, with those that have the spirit, will haste
To help Cominius.

TITUS LARTIUS

Worthy sir, thou bleed'st;
Thy exercise hath been too violent
For a second course of fight.

MARCIUS

Sir, praise me not;
My work hath yet not warm'd me. Fare you well;
The blood I drop is rather physical
Than dangerous to me. To Aufidius thus
I will appear, and fight.

1 ***come off*** **retired.**

TITUS LARTIUS

Now the fair goddess, Fortune,
Fall deep in love with thee, and her great charms
Misguide thy opposers' swords! Bold gentleman,
Prosperity be thy page!

MARCIUS

Thy friend no less
Than those she placeth highest! So farewell.

TITUS LARTIUS

Thou worthiest Marcius!

Exit MARCIUS

Go sound thy trumpet in the market-place;
Call thither all the officers o' th' town,
Where they shall know our mind. Away!

Exeunt

Scene six

Near the camp of Cominius.

Enter COMINIUS, *as if retreating, with* SOLDIERS.

COMINIUS

Breathe you, my friends. Well fought; we are come off
Like Romans, neither foolish in our stands
Nor cowardly in retire. Believe me, sirs,
We shall be charg'd again. Whiles we have struck,
By interims and conveying gusts we have heard
The charges of our friends. The Roman gods,
Lead their successes as we wish our own,

8 ***That both our powers … encountr'ing*** that both sections of our army will be smiling when they meet again (i.e. having both been victorious).

10 ***issued*** have come out/rallied.

17 ***confound*** waste.

That both our powers, with smiling fronts
encount'ring,
May give you thankful sacrifice!

Enter a MESSENGER.

Thy news?

MESSENGER

The citizens of Corioli have issued
And given to Lartius and to Marcius battle;
I saw our party to their trenches driven,
And then I came away.

COMINIUS

Though thou speak'st truth,
Methinks thou speak'st not well. How long is't
since?

MESSENGER

Above an hour, my lord.

COMINIUS

'Tis not a mile; briefly we heard their drums.
How couldst thou in a mile confound an hour,
And bring thy news so late?

MESSENGER

Spies of the Volsces
Held me in chase, that I was forc'd to wheel
Three or four miles about; else had I, sir,
Half an hour since brought my report.

Enter MARCIUS.

COMINIUS

Who's yonder

25 ***a tabor*** small drum.

29 ***clip*** clasp.

That does appear as he were flay'd? O gods!
He has the stamp of Marcius, and I have
Before-time seen him thus.

MARCIUS

Come I too late?

COMINIUS

The shepherd knows not thunder from a tabor
More than I know the sound of Marcius' tongue
From every meaner man.

MARCIUS

Come I too late?

COMINIUS

Ay, if you come not in the blood of others,
But mantled in your own.

MARCIUS

O! let me clip ye
In arms as sound as when I woo'd, in heart
As merry as when our nuptial day was done,
And tapers burn'd to bedward.

COMINIUS

Flower of warriors,
How is't with Titus Lartius?

MARCIUS

As with a man busied about decrees:
Condemning some to death and some to exile;
Ransoming him or pitying, threat'ning th' other;
Holding Corioli in the name of Rome
Even like a fawning greyhound in the leash,
To let him slip at will.

53 ***Antiates*** the soldiers of Antium.

55 ***very heart of hope*** the man on whom all their hopes are based.

COMINIUS

Where is that slave
Which told me they had beat you to your trenches?
Where is he? Call him hither.

MARCIUS

Let him alone;
He did inform the truth. But for our gentlemen,
The common file – a plague! tribunes for them!
The mouse ne'er shunn'd the cat as they did budge
From rascals worse than they.

COMINIUS

But how prevail'd you?

MARCIUS

Will the time serve to tell? I do not think.
Where is the enemy? Are you lords o' th' field?
If not, why cease you till you are so?

COMINIUS

Marcius,
We have at disadvantage fought, and did
Retire to win our purpose.

MARCIUS

How lies their battle? Know you on which side
They have plac'd their men of trust?

COMINIUS

As I guess, Marcius,
Their bands i' th' vaward are the Antiates,
Of their best trust; o'er them Aufidius,
Their very heart of hope.

67–75 ***If any such . . . Marcius*** in rallying the troops, Marcius gives a very clear picture of what honour means to him. It is one to place against the tribunes' estimation of his motives for fighting.

MARCIUS

I do beseech you,
By all the battles wherein we have fought,
By th' blood we have shed together, by th' vows
We have made to endure friends, that you
directly
Set me against Aufidius and his Antiates;
And that you not delay the present, but,
Filling the air with swords advanc'd and darts,
We prove this very hour.

COMINIUS

Though I could wish
You were conducted to a gentle bath
And balms applied to you, yet dare I never
Deny your asking: take your choice of those
That best can aid your action.

MARCIUS

Those are they
That most are willing. If any such be here –
As it were sin to doubt – that love this painting
Wherein you see me smear'd; if any fear
Lesser his person than an ill report;
If any think brave death outweighs bad life
And that his country's dearer than himself;
Let him alone, or so many so minded,
Wave thus to express his disposition,
And follow Marcius.

They all shout and wave their swords, take him up in their arms and cast up their caps.

O, me alone! Make you a sword of me?
If these shows be not outward, which of you

83 ***As cause will be obey'd*** as events demand; as circumstances dictate.

86 ***Make good this ostentation*** fight as well as you promise to.

But is four Volsces? None of you but is
Able to bear against the great Aufidius
A shield as hard as his. A certain number,
Though thanks to all, must I select from all; the rest
Shall bear the business in some other fight,
As cause will be obey'd. Please you to march;
And four shall quickly draw out my command,
Which men are best inclin'd.

COMINIUS

March on, my fellows;
Make good this ostentation, and you shall
Divide in all with us.

Exeunt

Scene seven

The gates of Corioli.

TITUS LARTIUS, *having set a guard upon Corioli, going with drum and trumpet toward* COMINIUS *and* CAIUS MARCIUS, *enters with a* LIEUTENANT, *other* SOLDIERS, *and a* SCOUT.

TITUS LARTIUS

So, let the ports be guarded; keep your duties
As I have set them down. If I do send, dispatch
Those centuries to our aid; the rest will serve
For a short holding. If we lose the field
We cannot keep the town.

LIEUTENANT

Fear not our care, sir.

1 ***promise-breaker*** this oath gains dramatic irony from Marcius' later actions.

7 ***Halloa*** hunt with shouts.

hare accepted symbol of timidity.

TITUS LARTIUS

Hence, and shut your gates upon's.
Our guider, come; to th' Roman camp conduct us.

Exeunt

Scene eight

A field of battle between the Roman and the Volscian camps.

Alarum, as in battle. Enter MARCIUS *and* AUFIDIUS *from opposite sides.*

MARCIUS

I'll fight with none but thee, for I do hate thee
Worse than a promise-breaker.

AUFIDIUS

We hate alike:
Not Afric owns a serpent I abhor
More than thy fame and envy. Fix thy foot.

MARCIUS

Let the first budger die the other's slave,
And the gods doom him after!

AUFIDIUS

If I fly, Marcius,
Halloa me like a hare.

MARCIUS

Within these three hours, Tullus,
Alone I fought in your Corioli walls,
And made what work I pleas'd. 'Tis not my blood
Wherein thou seest me mask'd. For thy revenge
Wrench up thy power to th' highest.

11–12 ***Wert thou … progeny*** Aufidius is referring to the fact that the Romans claimed they were descended from the Trojan royal family. Hector had defeated the Greeks' attempt to take the city.

15 ***condemned seconds*** with your support, which I now condemn.

7 ***fusty plebians*** mouldy-smelling common people.

AUFIDIUS

Wert thou the Hector
That was the whip of your bragg'd progeny,
Thou shouldst not scape me here.

Here they fight, and certain Volsces come to the aid of AUFIDIUS. MARCIUS *fights till they are driven in breathless.*

Officious, and not valiant, you have sham'd me
In your condemned seconds.

Exeunt

Scene nine

The Roman camp.

Flourish. Alarum. A retreat is sounded. Enter, from one side, COMINIUS *with the* ROMANS; *from the other side,* MARCIUS, *with his arm in a scarf.*

COMINIUS

If I should tell thee o'er this thy day's work,
Thou't not believe thy deeds; but I'll report it
Where senators shall mingle tears with smiles;
Where great patricians shall attend, and shrug,
I' th' end admire; where ladies shall be frighted
And, gladly quak'd, hear more; where the dull tribunes,
That with the fusty plebeians hate thine honours,
Shall say against their hearts 'We thank the gods
Our Rome hath such a soldier'.
Yet cam'st thou to a morsel of this feast,
Having fully din'd before.

Enter TITUS LARTIUS, *with his power, from the pursuit.*

13 ***caparison*** a horse's trappings.

15 ***charter*** prerogative or right.

19–20 ***He that . . . mine act*** he who has carried out his intentions has accomplished more than I.

21 ***The grave of your deserving*** i.e. we will not allow you to hide your good deeds.

23 ***traducement*** slander.

31–2 ***Well might . . . death*** Cominius' warning will prove to be prophetic, given the treatment Marcius will receive in Rome.

TITUS LARTIUS

O General,
Here is the steed, we the caparison.
Hadst thou beheld –

MARCIUS

Pray now, no more; my mother,
Who has a charter to extol her blood,
When she does praise me grieves me. I have done
As you have done – that's what I can; induc'd
As you have been – that's for my country.
He that has but effected his good will
Hath overta'en mine act.

COMINIUS

You shall not be
The grave of your deserving; Rome must know
The value of her own. 'Twere a concealment
Worse than a theft, no less than a traducement,
To hide your doings and to silence that
Which, to the spire and top of praises vouch'd,
Would seem but modest. Therefore, I beseech
you,
In sign of what you are, not to reward
What you have done, before our army hear me.

MARCIUS

I have some wounds upon me, and they smart
To hear themselves rememb'red.

COMINIUS

Should they not,
Well might they fester 'gainst ingratitude
And tent themselves with death. Of all the
horses –

43–7 ***When drums . . . th' wars*** a very difficult passage to translate literally as Marcius, in his agitation, has become somewhat incoherent. The sense is 'when soldiers in the field resort to flattery, then cities will be filled with two-faced sycophants. When steely soldiers become as soft as the courtiers' fine clothes, then let ovations be made for a man's part in wars.' Essentially, he is repudiating the soldiers' praise, saying that such sentiments do not belong in the field of honour but in the more treacherous mouths of politicians. He is subtly upbraiding the common people for their false flattery of him and denying that he has given up his store of the treasure so that they can have more.

49 ***foil'd some debile wretch*** put to the sword some feeble wretch.

51–3 ***acclamations . . . lies*** exaggerated praise – as if I enjoyed having what little I have done being fattened up by lies.

Whereof we have ta'en good, and good store – of
all
The treasure in this field achiev'd and city,
We render you the tenth; to be ta'en forth
Before the common distribution at
Your only choice.

MARCIUS

I thank you, General,
But cannot make my heart consent to take
A bribe to pay my sword. I do refuse it,
And stand upon my common part with those
That have beheld the doing.

A long flourish. They all cry 'Marcius, Marcius!', cast up their caps and lances. COMINIUS *and* LARTIUS *stand.*

May these same instruments which you profane
Never sound more! When drums and trumpets
shall
I' th' field prove flatterers, let courts and cities
be
Made all of false-fac'd soothing. When steel
grows
Soft as the parasite's silk, let him be made
An overture for th' wars. No more, I say.
For that I have not wash'd my nose that bled,
Or foil'd some debile wretch, which without note
Here's many else have done, you shout me forth
In acclamations hyperbolical,
As if I lov'd my little should be dieted
In praises sauc'd with lies.

COMINIUS

Too modest are you;

72–3 ***To undercrest … power*** treat my new title as a crest and serve under it with honour.

More cruel to your good report than grateful
To us that give you truly. By your patience,
If 'gainst yourself you be incens'd, we'll put
you –
Like one that means his proper harm – in
manacles,
Then reason safely with you. Therefore be it
known,
As to us, to all the world, that Caius Marcius
Wears this war's garland; in token of the which,
My noble steed, known to the camp, I give him,
With all his trim belonging; and from this time,
For what he did before Corioli, call him
With all th' applause and clamour of the host,
Caius Marcius Coriolanus.
Bear th' addition nobly ever!

Flourish. Trumpets sound, and drums.

ALL

Caius Marcius Coriolanus!

CORIOLANUS

I will go wash;
And when my face is fair you shall perceive
Whether I blush or no. Howbeit, I thank you;
I mean to stride your steed, and at all times
To undercrest your good addition
To th' fairness of my power.

COMINIUS

So, to our tent;
Where, ere we do repose us, we will write
To Rome of our success. You, Titus Lartius,
Must to Corioli back. Send us to Rome

77 ***The best*** i.e. the leading citizens of Corioli.

90 ***By Jupiter, forgot!*** the ease with which Coriolanus abandons this plea for mercy is often quoted as an example of his limited humanity by those critics who see him as a tyrant.

The best, with whom we may articulate
For their own good and ours.

TITUS LARTIUS

I shall, my lord.

CORIOLANUS

The gods begin to mock me. I, that now
Refus'd most princely gifts, am bound to beg
Of my Lord General.

COMINIUS

Take't – 'tis yours; what is't?

CORIOLANUS

I sometime lay here in Corioli
At a poor man's house; he us'd me kindly.
He cried to me; I saw him prisoner;
But then Aufidius was within my view,
And wrath o'erwhelm'd my pity. I request you
To give my poor host freedom.

COMINIUS

O, well begg'd!
Were he the butcher of my son, he should
Be free as is the wind. Deliver him, Titus.

TITUS LARTIUS

Marcius, his name?

CORIOLANUS

By Jupiter, forgot!
I am weary ; yea, my memory is tir'd.
Have we no wine here?

COMINIUS

Go we to our tent.

2 ***on good condition*** on favourable terms.

12 ***emulation*** desire to equal him.

15 ***potch*** jab.

The blood upon your visage dries; 'tis time
It should be look'd to. Come.

Exeunt

Scene ten

The camp of the Volsces.

A *flourish. Cornets. Enter* TULLUS AUFIDIUS *bloody, with two or three* SOLDIERS.

AUFIDIUS

The town is ta'en.

1 SOLDIER

'Twill be deliver'd back on good condition.

AUFIDIUS

Condition!
I would I were a Roman; for I cannot,
Being a Volsce, be that I am. Condition?
What good condition can a treaty find
I' th' part that is at mercy? Five times, Marcius,
I have fought with thee; so often hast thou beat
me;
And wouldst do so, I think, should we encounter
As often as we eat. By th' elements,
If e'er again I meet him beard to beard,
He's mine or I am his. Mine emulation
Hath not that honour in't it had; for where
I thought to crush him in an equal force,
True sword to sword, I'll potch at him some way,
Or wrath or craft may get him.

26 ***hospitable canon*** the laws of hospitality. This oath will prove to be prophetic in his later dealings with Marcius.

1 SOLDIER

He's the devil.

AUFIDIUS

Bolder, though not so subtle. My valour's poison'd
With only suff'ring stain by him; for him
Shall fly out of itself. Nor sleep nor sanctuary,
Being naked, sick, nor fane nor Capitol,
The prayers of priests nor times of sacrifice,
Embarquements all of fury, shall lift up
Their rotten privilege and custom 'gainst
My hate to Marcius. Where I find him, were it
At home, upon my brother's guard, even there,
Against the hospitable canon, would I
Wash my fierce hand in's heart. Go you to th' city;
Learn how 'tis held, and what they are that must
Be hostages for Rome.

1 SOLDIER

Will not you go?

AUFIDIUS

I am attended at the cypress grove; I pray you –
'Tis south the city mills – bring me word thither
How the world goes, that to the pace of it
I may spur on my journey.

1 SOLDIER

I shall, sir.

Exeunt

Act 2: summary

In Rome, the tribunes and Menenius argue about Marcius. Volumnia and Virgilia enter and news of Marcius' victory is given. His ambitious mother is overjoyed and predicts his passage to the highest office, consulship, will be an easy one.

Marcius enters at the head of a procession, crowned by Cominius with the victory garland. He is uncomfortable at being so singled out for praise and shows humility by bowing before his mother. As they leave for the Senate, Volumnia again raises the notion of him becoming consul and he shows himself to be by no means reconciled to this, particularly as it will involve him having to supplicate the people for their votes. The tribunes watch his departure, aware that his election would mean an end to their power.

In the Senate House, Coriolanus is judged by the magistrates. The tribunes grudgingly accept his services to Rome, although Brutus warns again of his hatred of the people. Unable to accept praise, Coriolanus sulkily leaves and has to be recalled to be told of the Senate's acceptance of his nomination. Never the politician, he begs to be excused the custom of seeking the people's approval. At the urging of the tribunes, the Senate reject this request.

The citizens argue with each other about whether to give him their votes. They are aware of his valour but also recognise his contempt of them. Coriolanus enters and, sarcastically, begs them for their 'voices'. He refuses to show his wounds and scarcely hides his contempt, yet succeeds in his aim and leaves for the Capitol, confident of his election. The tribunes immediately round the crowd up and get them to reconsider their decision. True politicians, they go to great pains to ensure that they will be distanced from the mob's action in reversing its decision.

1 ***augurer*** a Roman official whose duty was to foretell events by interpreting omens.

Act Two

Scene one

Rome. A public place.

Enter MENENIUS, *with the two Tribunes of the people,* SICINIUS *and* BRUTUS.

MENENIUS

The augurer tells me we shall have news to-night.

BRUTUS

Good or bad?

MENENIUS

Not according to the prayer of the people, for they love not Marcius.

SICINIUS

Nature teaches beasts to know their friends.

MENENIUS

Pray you, who does the wolf love?

SICINIUS

The lamb.

MENENIUS

Ay, to devour him, as the hungry plebeians would the noble Marcius.

BRUTUS

He's a lamb indeed, that baes like a bear.

MENENIUS

He's a bear indeed, that lives like a lamb. You two are old men; tell me one thing that I shall ask you.

21–2 ***us o' th' right-hand file*** literally right-wing, but Menenius is also making an allusion to the tradition whereby the best soldiers were put into the right hand file of an army.

27–8 ***for a little thief ... patience*** a very small happening will prove a thief to rob you of a great deal of your patience.

BOTH TRIBUNES

Well, sir.

MENENIUS

In what enormity is Marcius poor in that you two have not in abundance?

BRUTUS

He's poor in no one fault, but stor'd with all.

SICINIUS

Especially in pride.

BRUTUS

And topping all others in boasting.

MENENIUS

This is strange now. Do you two know how you are censured here in the city – I mean of us o' th' right-hand file? Do you?

BOTH TRIBUNES

Why, how are we censur'd?

MENENIUS

Because you talk of pride now – will you not be angry?

BOTH TRIBUNES

Well, well, sir, well.

MENENIUS

Why, 'tis no great matter; for a very little thief of occasion will rob you of a great deal of patience. Give your dispositions the reins, and be angry at your pleasures – at the least, if you take it as a pleasure to you in being so. You blame Marcius for being proud?

36 ***wondrous single*** i.e. feeble.

48 ***allaying Tiber in't*** diluting water. The Tiber is the river on which Rome stands.

54 ***wealsmen*** i) men of the commonwealth; ii) men doing good for the commonwealth (irony).

55 ***Lycurguses*** the legendary law-giver of Sparta.

BRUTUS

We do it not alone, sir.

MENENIUS

I know you can do very little alone; for your helps are many, or else your actions would grow wondrous single: your abilities are too infant-like for doing much alone. You talk of pride. O that you could turn your eyes toward the napes of your necks, and make but an interior survey of your good selves! O that you could!

BOTH

What then, sir?

MENENIUS

Why, then you should discover a brace of unmeriting, proud, violent, testy magistrates – alias fools – as any in Rome.

SICINIUS

Menenius, you are known well enough too.

MENENIUS

I am known to be a humorous patrician, and one that loves a cup of hot wine with not a drop of allaying Tiber in't; said to be something imperfect in favouring the first complaint, hasty and tinder-like upon too trivial motion; one that converses more with the buttock of the night than with the forehead of the morning. What I think I utter, and spend my malice in my breath. Meeting two such wealsmen as you are – I cannot call you Lycurguses – if the drink you give me touch my palate adversely, I make a crooked face

58–9 ***the ass … syllables*** stupidity in most of what you say.

64–5 ***bisson conspectuities*** bleary-eyed insights.

71–2 ***orange-wife and a fosset-seller*** a woman who sells oranges and a man who sells pegs for barrels.

72 ***rejourn the controversy*** adjourn the case.

75–8 ***you make … bleeding*** you make grotesque faces, like a mime artist, encourage dispute rather than patience, and, in shouting out for a recess, leave the matter still unsettled.

83 ***giber for the table*** dinner table wit.

at it. I cannot say your worships have deliver'd the matter well, when I find the ass in compound with the major part of your syllables; and though I must be content to bear with those that say you are reverend grave men, yet they lie deadly that tell you you have good faces. If you see this in the map of my microcosm, follows it that I am known well enough too? What harm can your bisson conspectuities glean out of this character, if I be known well enough too?

BRUTUS

Come, sir, come, we know you well enough.

MENENIUS

You know neither me, yourselves, nor any thing. You are ambitious for poor knaves' caps and legs; you wear out a good wholesome forenoon in hearing a cause between an orange-wife and a fosset-seller, and then rejourn the controversy of threepence to a second day of audience. When you are hearing a matter between party and party, if you chance to be pinch'd with the colic, you make faces like mummers, set up the bloody flag against all patience, and, in roaring for a chamber-pot, dismiss the controversy bleeding, the more entangled by your hearing. All the peace you make in their cause is calling both the parties knaves. You are a pair of strange ones.

BRUTUS

Come, come, you are well understood to be a perfecter giber for the table than a necessary bencher in the Capitol.

90 ***botcher's*** a botcher was a patcher of clothes.

93 ***Deucalion*** the story of Deucalion was the Roman equivalent of Noah and the Flood.

MENENIUS

Our very priests must become mockers, if they shall encounter such ridiculous subjects as you are. When you speak best unto the purpose, it is not worth the wagging of your beards; and your beards deserve not so honourable a grave as to stuff a botcher's cushion or to be entomb'd in an ass's pack-saddle. Yet you must be saying Marcius is proud; who, in a cheap estimation, is worth all your predecessors since Deucalion; though peradventure some of the best of 'em were hereditary hangmen. God-den to your worships. More of your conversation would infect my brain, being the herdsmen of the beastly plebeians. I will be bold to take my leave of you.

BRUTUS *and* SICINIUS *go aside.*

Enter VOLUMNIA, VIRGILIA, *and* VALERIA.

How now, my as fair as noble ladies – and the moon, were she earthly, no nobler – whither do you follow your eyes so fast?

VOLUMNIA

Honourable Menenius, my boy Marcius approaches; for the love of Juno let's go.

MENENIUS

Ha! Marcius coming home?

VOLUMNIA

Ay, worthy Menenius, and with most prosperous approbation.

120 ***Galen*** a famous Roman healer.

empiricutic quackery; fake medicine.

121 ***horse-drench*** draught of horse medicine.

MENENIUS

Take my cap, Jupiter, and I thank thee. Hoo! Marcius coming home!

VOLUMNIA AND VIRGILIA

Nay, 'tis true.

VOLUMNIA

Look, here's a letter from him; the state hath another, his wife another; and I think there's one at home for you.

MENENIUS

I will make my very house reel to-night. A letter for me?

VIRGILIA

Yes, certain, there's a letter for you; I saw't.

MENENIUS

A letter for me! It gives me an estate of seven years' health; in which time I will make a lip at the physician. The most sovereign prescription in Galen is but empiricutic and, to this preservative, of no better report than a horse-drench. Is he not wounded? He was wont to come home wounded.

VIRGILIA

O, no, no, no.

VOLUMNIA

O, he is wounded, I thank the gods for't.

MENENIUS

So do I too, if it be not too much. Brings 'a victory in his pocket? The wounds become him.

134 ***fidius'd*** Menenius is making a pun on the name of Aufidius. The meaning is unclear.

145 ***pow wow*** an expression of scorn.

VOLUMNIA

On's brows, Menenius, he comes the third time home with the oaken garland.

MENENIUS

Has he disciplin'd Aufidius soundly?

VOLUMNIA

Titus Lartius writes they fought together, but Aufidius got off.

MENENIUS

And 'twas time for him too, I'll warrant him that; an he had stay'd by him, I would not have been so fidius'd for all the chests in Corioli and the gold that's in them. Is the Senate possess'd of this?

VOLUMNIA

Good ladies, let's go. Yes, yes, yes: the Senate has letters from the General, wherein he gives my son the whole name of the war; he hath in this action outdone his former deeds doubly.

VALERIA

In troth, there's wondrous things spoke of him.

MENENIUS

Wondrous! Ay, I warrant you, and not without his true purchasing.

VIRGILIA

The gods grant them true!

VOLUMNIA

True! pow, wow.

151 ***cicatrices*** scars.

153 ***Tarquin*** the last king of Rome, defeated as Rome became a republic.

160–3 ***These are ... men die*** Volumnia equates Marcius with death. This image will be repeated throughout the play and will develop until he is dehumanised, becoming a machine of destruction.

MENENIUS

True! I'll be sworn they are true. Where is he wounded? (*To the* TRIBUNES) God save your good worships! Marcius is coming home; he has more cause to be proud. Where is he wounded?

VOLUMNIA

I' th' shoulder and i' th' left arm; there will be large cicatrices to show the people when he shall stand for his place. He received in the repulse of Tarquin seven hurts i' th' body.

MENENIUS

One i' th' neck and two i' th' thigh – there's nine that I know.

VOLUMNIA

He had before this last expedition twenty-five wounds upon him.

MENENIUS

Now it's twenty-seven; every gash was an enemy's grave. (*A shout and flourish*) Hark! the trumpets.

VOLUMNIA

These are the ushers of Marcius. Before him he carries noise, and behind him he leaves tears;
Death, that dark spirit, in's nervy arm doth lie,
Which, being advanc'd, declines, and then men die.

A sennet. Trumpets sound. Enter COMINIUS *the General, and* TITUS LARTIUS; *between them,* MARCIUS, *crowned with an oak garland; with* CAPTAINS *and* SOLDIERS *and a* HERALD.

166 ***With fame . . . Marcius*** along with fame, a name in addition to Caius Marcius.

HERALD

Know, Rome, that all alone Marcius did fight
Within Corioli gates, where he hath won,
With fame, a name to Caius Marcius; these
In honour follows Coriolanus.
Welcome to Rome, renowned Coriolanus!

Flourish.

ALL

Welcome to Rome, renowned Coriolanus!

CORIOLANUS

No more of this, it does offend my heart.
Pray now, no more.

COMINIUS

Look, sir, your mother!

CORIOLANUS

O,
You have, I know, petition'd all the gods
For my prosperity! (*Kneels*)

VOLUMNIA

Nay, my good soldier, up;
My gentle Marcius, worthy Caius, and
By deed-achieving honour newly nam'd –
What is it? Coriolanus must I call thee?
But, O, thy wife!

CORIOLANUS

My gracious silence, hail!
Wouldst thou have laugh'd had I come coffin'd home,
That weep'st to see me triumph? Ah, my dear,

191–2 ***We have ... relish*** the tribunes are pictured as sour crab apple trees which resist being improved by being grafted to a finer species.

193–4 ***We call ... folly*** Menenius can afford to be so scornful as Coriolanus is in the ascendancy, yet when the tribunes wield their power we see that the patrician class do not speak so forthrightly, instead depending upon policy. This is to be a key element in Coriolanus' fall.

Such eyes the widows in Corioli wear,
And mothers that lack sons.

MENENIUS

Now the gods crown thee!

CORIOLANUS

And live you yet? (*To* VALERIA) O my sweet lady,
pardon.

VOLUMNIA

I know not where to turn.
O, welcome home! And welcome, General.
And y'are welcome all.

MENENIUS

A hundred thousand welcomes. I could weep
And I could laugh; I am light and heavy. Welcome!
A curse begin at very root on's heart
That is not glad to see thee! You are three
That Rome should dote on; yet, by the faith of
men,
We have some old crab trees here at home that
will not
Be grafted to your relish. Yet welcome, warriors.
We call a nettle but a nettle, and
The faults of fools but folly.

COMINIUS

Ever right.

CORIOLANUS

Menenius ever, ever.

HERALD

Give way there, and go on.

210–13 ***kitchen malkin . . . eye him*** the kitchen maid pins her finest linen around her greasy neck and climbs walls to glimpse him.

CORIOLANUS

(*To his wife and mother*) Your hand, and yours.
Ere in our own house I do shade my head,
The good patricians must be visited;
From whom I have receiv'd not only greetings,
But with them change of honours.

VOLUMNIA

I have lived
To see inherited my very wishes,
And the buildings of my fancy; only
There's one thing wanting, which I doubt not but
Our Rome will cast upon thee.

CORIOLANUS

Know, good mother,
I had rather be their servant in my way
Than sway with them in theirs.

COMINIUS

On, to the Capitol.

Flourish. Cornets. Exeunt in state, as before

BRUTUS *and* SICINIUS *come forward.*

BRUTUS

All tongues speak of him and the bleared sights
Are spectacled to see him. Your prattling nurse
Into a rapture lets her baby cry
While she chats him; the kitchen malkin pins
Her richest lockram 'bout her reechy neck,
Clamb'ring the walls to eye him; stalls, bulks, windows,
Are smother'd up, leads fill'd and ridges hors'd

215 ***flamens*** priests rarely seen in public.

217–20 ***our veiled . . . kisses*** the reference picks up the Elizabethan fashion for pale skins. Here the women who have gone to such great lengths to hide their faces from the sun, risk their complexions to get a better view of him.

231–33 ***which . . . do't*** which cause I have no doubt he will give them, taking into consideration his pride.

With variable complexions, all agreeing
In earnestness to see him. Seld-shown flamens
Do press among the popular throngs and puff
To win a vulgar station; our veil'd dames
Commit the war of white and damask in
Their nicely gawded cheeks to th' wanton spoil
Of Phœbus' burning kisses. Such a pother,
As if that whatsoever god who leads him
Were slily crept into his human powers,
And gave him graceful posture.

SICINIUS

On the sudden
I warrant him consul.

BRUTUS

Then our office may
During his power go sleep.

SICINIUS

He cannot temp'rately transport his honours
From where he should begin and end, but will
Lose those he hath won.

BRUTUS

In that there's comfort.

SICINIUS

Doubt not
The commoners, for whom we stand, but they
Upon their ancient malice will forget
With the least cause these his new honours; which
That he will give them make I as little question
As he is proud to do't.

236 ***vesture of humility*** a traditional ritual was for the man accepted by the Senate as consul to have to appear before the people humbly to seek their approval.

BRUTUS

I heard him swear,
Were he to stand for consul, never would he
Appear i' th' market-place, nor on him put
The napless vesture of humility;
Nor, showing, as the manner is, his wounds
To th' people, beg their stinking breaths.

SICINIUS

'Tis right.

BRUTUS

It was his word. O, he would miss it rather
Than carry it but by the suit of the gentry to him
And the desire of the nobles.

SICINIUS

I wish no better
Than have him hold that purpose, and to put it
In execution.

BRUTUS

'Tis most like he will.

SICINIUS

It shall be to him then as our good wills:
A sure destruction.

BRUTUS

So it must fall out
To him or our authorities. For an end,
We must suggest the people in what hatred
He still hath held them; that to's power he would
Have made them mules, silenc'd their pleaders, and
Dispropertied their freedoms; holding them

253 ***provand*** food.

In human action and capacity
Of no more soul nor fitness for the world
Than camels in their war, who have their
provand
Only for bearing burdens, and sore blows
For sinking under them.

SICINIUS

This, as you say, suggested
At some time when his soaring insolence
Shall touch the people – which time shall not
want,
If he be put upon't, and that's as easy
As to set dogs on sheep – will be his fire
To kindle their dry stubble; and their blaze
Shall darken him for ever.

Enter a MESSENGER.

BRUTUS

What's the matter?

MESSENGER

You are sent for to the Capitol. 'Tis thought
That Marcius shall be consul.
I have seen the dumb men throng to see him
and
The blind to hear him speak; matrons flung
gloves,
Ladies and maids their scarfs and handkerchers,
Upon him as he pass'd; the nobles bended
As to Jove's statue, and the commons made
A shower and thunder with their caps and
shouts.
I never saw the like.

271–2 ***And carry with us . . . event*** i.e. let us look like we are part of the celebrations yet stay faithful to what we intend to do.

3 ***Three*** we never see nor hear of the other two.

BRUTUS

Let's to the Capitol,
And carry with us ears and eyes for th' time,
But hearts for the event.

SICINIUS

Have with you.

Exeunt

Scene two

Rome. The Capitol.

Enter two OFFICERS, *to lay cushions.*

1 OFFICER

Come, come, they are almost here. How many stand for consulships?

2 OFFICER

Three, they say; but 'tis thought of every one Coriolanus will carry it.

1 OFFICER

That's a brave fellow; but he's vengeance proud and loves not the common people.

2 OFFICER

Faith, there have been many great men that have flatter'd the people, who ne'er loved them; and there be many that they have loved, they know not wherefore; so that, if they love they know not why, they hate upon no better a ground. Therefore, for Coriolanus neither to care whether they love or hate him manifests the true knowledge he

21–2 ***Now to seem to affect*** to give the impression of preferring.

26–9 ***those who . . . report*** those who, through being courteous and obsequious to the people, have gained popularity and good reputations without having done anything else to deserve them.

has in their disposition, and out of his noble carelessness lets them plainly see't.

1 OFFICER
If he did not care whether he had their love or no, he waved indifferently 'twixt doing them neither good nor harm; but he seeks their hate with greater devotion than they can render it him, and leaves nothing undone that may fully discover him their opposite. Now to seem to affect the malice and displeasure of the people is as bad as that which he dislikes – to flatter them for their love.

2 OFFICER
He hath deserved worthily of his country; and his ascent is not by such easy degrees as those who, having been supple and courteous to the people, bonneted, without any further deed to have them at all, into their estimation and report; but he hath so planted his honours in their eyes and his actions in their hearts that for their tongues to be silent and not confess so much were a kind of ingrateful injury; to report otherwise were a malice that, giving itself the lie, would pluck reproof and rebuke from every ear that heard it.

1 OFFICER
No more of him; he's a worthy man. Make way, they are coming.

A Sennet. Enter the PATRICIANS *and the* TRIBUNES *of the People,* LICTORS *before them;* CORIOLANUS, MENENIUS, COMINIUS *the Consul.* SICINIUS *and* BRUTUS *take their places by themselves.* CORIOLANUS *stands.*

51–2 ***Rather our . . . it out*** that Rome has not the means to reward such service rather than we are unwilling to strain to find a way.

MENENIUS

Having determin'd of the Volsces, and
To send for Titus Lartius, it remains,
As the main point of this our after-meeting,
To gratify his noble service that
Hath thus stood for his country. Therefore
please you,
Most reverend and grave elders, to desire
The present consul and last general
In our well-found successes to report
A little of that worthy work perform'd
By Caius Marcius Coriolanus; whom
We met here both to thank and to remember
With honours like himself.

CORIOLANUS *sits.*

1 SENATOR

Speak, good Cominius.
Leave nothing out for length, and make us think
Rather our state's defective for requital
Than we to stretch it out. Masters o' th' people,
We do request your kindest ears and, after,
Your loving motion toward the common body,
To yield what passes here.

SICINIUS

We are convented
Upon a pleasing treaty, and have hearts
Inclinable to honour and advance
The theme of our assembly.

BRUTUS

Which the rather
We shall be bless'd to do, if he remember

60 ***A kinder value*** a higher value.

66 ***tie him not ... bedfellow*** do not expect him to love them.

A kinder value of the people than
He hath hereto priz'd them at.

MENENIUS

That's off, that's off;
I would you rather had been silent. Please you
To hear Cominius speak?

BRUTUS

Most willingly.
But yet my caution was more pertinent
Than the rebuke you give it.

MENENIUS

He loves your people;
But tie him not to be their bedfellow.
Worthy Cominius, speak.

CORIOLANUS *rises, and offers to go away.*

Nay, keep your place.

1 SENATOR
Sit, Coriolanus, never shame to hear
What you have nobly done.

CORIOLANUS

Your Honours' pardon.
I had rather have my wounds to heal again
Than hear say how I got them.

BRUTUS

Sir, I hope
My words disbench'd you not.

CORIOLANUS

No, sir; yet oft,

88 ***singly counterpois'd*** equalled by one other person.

When blows have made me stay, I fled from words.
You sooth'd not, therefore hurt not. But your people,
I love them as they weigh –

MENENIUS

Pray now, sit down.

CORIOLANUS

I had rather have one scratch my head i' th' sun
When the alarum were struck than idly sit
To hear my nothings monster'd.

Exit

MENENIUS

Masters of the people,
Your multiplying spawn how can he flatter –
That's thousand to one good one – when you now see
He had rather venture all his limbs for honour
Than one on's ears to hear it? Proceed, Cominius.

COMINIUS

I shall lack voice; the deeds of Coriolanus
Should not be utter'd feebly. It is held
That valour is the chiefest virtue and
Most dignifies the haver. If it be,
The man I speak of cannot in the world
Be singly counterpois'd. At sixteen years,
When Tarquin made a head for Rome, he fought
Beyond the mark of others; our then Dictator,
Whom with all praise I point at, saw him fight

92 ***Amazonian chin*** the Amazons were a tribe of women warriors. Coriolanus is compared to them because, being so young, he too had no facial hair.

97 ***might act the woman … scene*** i.e. might have been expected to weep at the sights of war.

118 ***Re-quick'ned … fatigate*** revived his tired body.

121 ***perpetual spoil*** an endless hunt. The image suggests the delight of Coriolanus in what he sees as a game.

When with his Amazonian chin he drove
The bristled lips before him; he bestrid
An o'erpress'd Roman and i' th' consul's view
Slew three opposers; Tarquin's self he met,
And struck him on his knee. In that day's feats,
When he might act the woman in the scene,
He prov'd best man i' th' field, and for his meed
Was brow-bound with the oak. His pupil age
Man-ent'red thus, he waxed like a sea,
And in the brunt of seventeen battles since
He lurch'd all swords of the garland. For this last,
Before and in Corioli, let me say
I cannot speak him home. He stopp'd the fliers,
And by his rare example made the coward
Turn terror into sport; as weeds before
A vessel under sail, so men obey'd
And fell below his stem. His sword, death's
  stamp,
Where it did mark, it took; from face to foot
He was a thing of blood, whose every motion
Was tim'd with dying cries. Alone he ent'red
The mortal gate of th' city, which he painted
With shunless destiny; aidless came off,
And with a sudden re-enforcement struck
Corioli like a planet. Now all's his.
When by and by the din of war 'gan pierce
His ready sense, then straight his doubled spirit
Re-quick'ned what in flesh was fatigate,
And to the battle came he; where he did
Run reeking o'er the lives of men, as if
'Twere a perpetual spoil; and till we call'd
Both field and city ours he never stood
To ease his breast with panting.

130 ***To spend the time . . . it*** i.e. feels that time well spent is an end in itself.

MENENIUS

Worthy man!

1 SENATOR

He cannot but with measure fit the honours
Which we devise him.

COMINIUS

Our spoils he kick'd at,
And look'd upon things precious as they were
The common muck of the world. He covets less
Than misery itself would give, rewards
His deeds with doing them, and is content
To spend the time to end it.

MENENIUS

He's right noble;
Let him be call'd for.

1 SENATOR

Call Coriolanus.

OFFICER

He doth appear.

Re-enter CORIOLANUS.

MENENIUS

The Senate, Coriolanus, are well pleas'd
To make thee consul.

CORIOLANUS

I do owe them still
My life and services.

MENENIUS

It then remains
That you do speak to the people.

142 ***Put them not to't*** do not push them into a confrontation over this.

146–7 ***and might well ... people*** Coriolanus' lack of political astuteness is revealed by such a contentious statement being made in public.

CORIOLANUS

I do beseech you
Let me o'erleap that custom; for I cannot
Put on the gown, stand naked, and entreat them
For my wounds' sake to give their suffrage.
Please you
That I may pass this doing.

SICINIUS

Sir, the people
Must have their voices; neither will they bate
One jot of ceremony.

MENENIUS

Put them not to't.
Pray you go fit you to the custom, and
Take to you, as your predecessors have,
Your honour with your form.

CORIOLANUS

It is a part
That I shall blush in acting, and might well
Be taken from the people.

BRUTUS

Mark you that?

CORIOLANUS

To brag unto them 'Thus I did, and thus!'
Show them th' unaching scars which I should hide,
As if I had receiv'd them for the hire
Of their breath only!

MENENIUS

Do not stand upon't.

153 ***purpose*** proposal.

157–9 ***He will require . . . give*** a difficult sentence. Sicinius is prophesying that Coriolanus will demand the people's vote in a way which will show how disdainful he is that they should have it in the first place.

We recommend to you, Tribunes of the People,
Our purpose to them; and to our noble consul
Wish we all joy and honour.

SENATOR

To Coriolanus come all joy and honour!

Flourish. Cornets. Then exeunt all but SICINIUS *and* BRUTUS

BRUTUS

You see how he intends to use the people.

SICINIUS

May they perceive's intent! He will require them
As if he did comtemn what he requested
Should be in them to give.

BRUTUS

Come, we'll inform them
Of our proceedings here. On th' market-place
I know they do attend us.

Exeunt

Scene three

Rome. The Forum.

Enter seven or eight CITIZENS.

1 CITIZEN

Once, if he do require our voices, we ought not to deny him.

2 CITIZEN

We may, sir, if we will.

6–8 ***we are to put . . . for them*** the citizen feels that the wounds Coriolanus has received for his country require reward, which in this case is to be the people's agreement to his election.

16 ***stuck not*** did not hesitate.

3 CITIZEN

We have power in ourselves to do it, but it is a power that we have no power to do; for if he show us his wounds and tell us his deeds, we are to put our tongues into those wounds and speak for them; so, if he tell us his noble deeds, we must also tell him our noble acceptance of them. Ingratitude is monstrous, and for the multitude to be ingrateful were to make a monster of the multitude; of the which we being members should bring ourselves to be monstrous members.

1 CITIZEN

And to make us no better thought of, a little help will serve; for once we stood up about the corn, he himself stuck not to call us the many-headed multitude.

3 CITIZEN

We have been call'd so of many; not that our heads are some brown, some black, some abram, some bald, but that our wits are so diversely colour'd; and truly I think if all our wits were to issue out of one skull, they would fly east, west, north, south, and their consent of one direct way should be at once to all the points o' th' compass.

2 CITIZEN

Think you so? Which way do you judge my wit would fly?

3 CITIZEN

Nay, your wit will not so soon out as another man's will – 'tis strongly wedg'd up in a block-

48 ***single honour*** individual right.

head; but if it were at liberty 'twould sure southward.

2 CITIZEN
Why that way?

3 CITIZEN
To lose itself in a fog; where being three parts melted away with rotten dews, the fourth would return for conscience' sake, to help to get thee a wife.

2 CITIZEN
You are never without your tricks; you may, you may.

3 CITIZEN
Are you all resolv'd to give your voices? But that's no matter, the greater part carries it. I say, if he would incline to the people, there was never a worthier man.

Enter CORIOLANUS, *in a gown of humility, with* MENENIUS.

Here he comes, and in the gown of humility. Mark his behaviour. We are not to stay all together, but to come by him where he stands, by ones, by twos, and by threes. He's to make his requests by particulars, wherein every one of us has a single honour, in giving him our own voices with our own tongues; therefore follow me, and I'll direct you how you shall go by him.

ALL
Content, content.

Exeunt CITIZENS

61–2 ***like the virtues . . . 'em*** as they forget the virtues preached to them by our priests.

65 ***a brace*** a pair; two – he is using an animal image and so his scorn is apparent.

MENENIUS

O sir, you are not right; have you not known
The worthiest men have done't?

CORIOLANUS

What must I say?
'I pray, sir' – Plague upon't! I cannot bring
My tongue to such a pace. 'Look, sir, my wounds!
I got them in my country's service, when
Some certain of your brethren roar'd, and ran
From th' noise of our own drums.'

MENENIUS

O me, the gods!
You must not speak of that. You must desire them
To think upon you.

CORIOLANUS

Think upon me? Hang 'em!
I would they would forget me, like the virtues
Which our divines lose by 'em.

MENENIUS

You'll mar all.
I'll leave you. Pray you speak to 'em, I pray you,
In wholesome manner.

Exit

Re-enter three of the CITIZENS.

CORIOLANUS

Bid them wash their faces
And keep their teeth clean. So, here comes a brace.
You know the cause, sir, of my standing here.

69 ***Your own desert?*** within this question one can sense the surprise of the citizen at the abruptness of the previous answer – he is clearly used to talking to more politically astute candidates for office!

3 CITIZEN
We do, sir; tell us what hath brought you to't.

CORIOLANUS
Mine own desert.

2 CITIZEN
Your own desert?

CORIOLANUS
Ay, not mine own desire.

3 CITIZEN
How, not your own desire?

CORIOLANUS
No, sir, 'twas never my desire yet to trouble the poor with begging.

3 CITIZEN
You must think, if we give you anything, we hope to gain by you.

CORIOLANUS
Well then, I pray, your price o' th' consulship?

1 CITIZEN
The price is to ask it kindly.

CORIOLANUS
Kindly, sir, I pray let me ha't. I have wounds to show you, which shall be yours in private. Your good voice, sir; what say you?

2 CITIZEN
You shall ha' it, worthy sir.

85 ***An 'twere*** if it were.

92 ***Your enigma?*** i.e. the meaning of your puzzle.

CORIOLANUS

A match, sir. There's in all two worthy voices begg'd. I have your alms. Adieu.

3 CITIZEN

But this is something odd.

2 CITIZEN

An 'twere to give again – but 'tis no matter.

Exeunt the three CITIZENS

Re-enter two other CITIZENS.

CORIOLANUS

Pray you now, if it may stand with the tune of your voices that I may be consul, I have here the customary gown.

4 CITIZEN

You have deserved nobly of your country, and you have not deserved nobly.

CORIOLANUS

Your enigma?

4 CITIZEN

You have been a scourge to her enemies; you have been a rod to her friends. You have not indeed loved the common people.

CORIOLANUS

You should account me the more virtuous, that I have not been common in my love. I will, sir, flatter my sworn brother, the people, to earn a dearer estimation of them; 'tis a condition they account gentle; and since the wisdom of their

102–4 ***I will . . . desirers*** I will lay on thick my liking for the commoner for whoever wants me to.

117 ***Hob and Dick*** no matter whom, i.e. Tom, Dick and Harry.

118 ***needless vouchers*** unnecessary votes. It is clear that he sees this as ritual only and underestimates its importance.

120–2 ***The dust . . . o'erpeer*** it is his belief that tradition allows wrongs to be cloaked and thus go unchanged.

choice is rather to have my hat than my heart, I will practise the insinuating nod and be off to them most counterfeitly. That is, sir, I will counterfeit the bewitchment of some popular man and give it bountiful to the desirers. Therefore, beseech you I may be consul.

5 CITIZEN

We hope to find you our friend; and therefore give you our voices heartily.

4 CITIZEN

You have received many wounds for your country.

CORIOLANUS

I will not seal your knowledge with showing them. I will make much of your voices, and so trouble you no farther.

BOTH CITIZENS

The gods give you joy, sir, heartily!

Exeunt CITIZENS

CORIOLANUS

Most sweet voices!
Better it is to die, better to starve,
Than crave the hire which first we do deserve.
Why in this wolvish toge should I stand here
To beg of Hob and Dick that do appear
Their needless vouches? Custom calls me to't.
What custom wills, in all things should we do't,
The dust on antique time would lie unswept,
And mountainous error be too highly heap'd
For truth to o'erpeer. Rather than fool it so,
Let the high office and the honour go

139 ***stood your limitation*** i.e. the time required of you.

To one that would do thus. I am half through:
The one part suffered, the other will I do.

Re-enter three more CITIZENS.

Here come more voices.
Your voices. For your voices I have fought;
Watch'd for your voices; for your voices bear
Of wounds two dozen odd; battles thrice six
I have seen and heard of; for your voices have
Done many things, some less, some more. Your
voices?
Indeed, I would be consul.

6 CITIZEN

He has done nobly, and cannot go without any honest man's voice.

7 CITIZEN

Therefore let him be consul. The gods give him joy, and make him good friend to the people!

ALL

Amen, amen. God save thee, noble consul!

Exeunt CITIZENS

CORIOLANUS

Worthy voices!

Re-enter MENENIUS *with* BRUTUS *and* SICINIUS.

MENENIUS

You have stood your limitation, and the tribunes
Endue you with the people's voice. Remains
That, in th' official marks invested, you
Anon do meet the Senate.

145 ***upon your approbation*** to formalise approval of you.

CORIOLANUS

Is this done?

SICINIUS

The custom of request you have discharg'd.
The people do admit you, and are summon'd
To meet anon, upon your approbation.

CORIOLANUS

Where? At the Senate House?

SICINIUS

There, Coriolanus.

CORIOLANUS

May I change these garments?

SICINIUS

You may, sir.

CORIOLANUS

That I'll straight do, and, knowing myself again,
Repair to th' Senate House.

MENENIUS

I'll keep you company. Will you along?

BRUTUS

We stay here for the people.

SICINIUS

Fare you well.

Exeunt CORIOLANUS AND MENENIUS

He has it now; and by his looks methinks
'Tis warm at's heart.

160 ***flouted*** disdained; ridiculed.

165 ***Why so . . . sure*** notice the way in which the tribune incites the mob.

BRUTUS

With a proud heart he wore
His humble weeds. Will you dismiss the people?

Re-enter CITIZENS.

SICINIUS

How now, my masters! Have you chose this man?

1 CITIZEN

He has our voices, sir.

BRUTUS

We pray the gods he may deserve your loves.

2 CITIZEN

Amen, sir. To my poor unworthy notice,
He mock'd us when he begg'd our voices.

3 CITIZEN

Certainly;
He flouted us downright.

1 CITIZEN

No, 'tis his kind of speech – he did not mock us.

2 CITIZEN

Not one amongst us, save yourself, but says
He us'd us scornfully. He should have show'd us
His marks of merit, wounds receiv'd for's country.

SICINIUS

Why, so he did, I am sure.

ALL

No, no; no man saw 'em.

182 ***body of the weal*** the commonwealth.

3 CITIZEN

He said he had wounds which he could show in private,
And with his hat, thus waving it in scorn,
'I would be consul;' says he 'aged custom
But by your voices will not so permit me;
Your voices therefore'. When we granted that,
Here was 'I thank you for your voices. Thank you,
Your most sweet voices. Now you have left your voices,
I have no further with you'. Was not this mockery?

SICINIUS

Why either were you ignorant to see't,
Or, seeing it, of such childish friendliness
To yield your voices?

BRUTUS

Could you not have told him –
As you were lesson'd – when he had no power
But was a petty servant to the state,
He was your enemy; ever spake against
Your liberties and the charters that you bear
I' th' body of the weal; and now, arriving
A place of potency and sway o' th' state,
If he should still malignantly remain
Fast foe to th' plebeii, your voices might
Be curses to yourselves? You should have said
That as his worthy deeds did claim no less
Than what he stood for so his gracious nature
Would think upon you for your voices, and
Translate his malice towards you into love,
Standing your friendly lord.

199 ***choler*** anger.

206 ***the rectorship of judgment*** the rule of Reason.

SICINIUS

Thus to have said,
As you were fore-advis'd, had touch'd his spirit
And tried his inclination; from him pluck'd
Either his gracious promise, which you might,
As cause had call'd you up, have held him to;
Or else it would have gall'd his surly nature,
Which easily endures not article
Tying him to aught. So, putting him to rage,
You should have ta'en th' advantage of his choler
And pass'd him unelected.

BRUTUS

Did you perceive
He did solicit you in free contempt
When he did need your loves; and do you think
That his contempt shall not be bruising to you
When he hath power to crush? Why, had your bodies
No heart among you? Or had you tongues to cry
Against the rectorship of judgment?

SICINIUS

Have you
Ere now denied the asker, and now again,
Of him that did not ask but mock, bestow
Your su'd-for tongues?

3 CITIZEN

He's not confirm'd: we may deny him yet.

2 CITIZEN

And will deny him;
I'll have five hundred voices of that sound.

225 ***portance*** bearing.

228 ***labour'd . . . impediment*** urged that nothing should stand in the way. The tribunes are astute enough to hide their role in the decision until victory has been assured.

1 CITIZEN
I twice five hundred, and their friends to piece
'em.

BRUTUS
Get you hence instantly, and tell those friends
They have chose a consul that will from them
take
Their liberties, make them of no more voice
Than dogs, that are often beat for barking
As therefore kept to do so.

SICINIUS
Let them assemble;
And, on a safer judgment, all revoke
Your ignorant election. Enforce his pride
And his old hate unto you; besides, forget not
With what contempt he wore the humble weed;
How in his suit he scorn'd you; but your loves,
Thinking upon his services, took from you
Th' apprehension of his present portance,
Which, most gibingly, ungravely, he did fashion
After the inveterate hate he bears you.

BRUTUS
Lay
A fault on us, your tribunes, that we labour'd,
No impediment between, but that you must
Cast your election on him.

SICINIUS
Say you chose him
More after our commandment than as guided
By your own true affections; and that your
minds,

240–1 ***Ancus Marcius . . . Numa . . . Hostilius*** all are previous kings of Rome. Brutus is, of course, adding weight to his accusation that Coriolanus has dictatorial aspirations by stressing his regal ancestors. Do not forget that Rome was a republic, having defeated its monarchy!

244 ***Censorinus*** a Roman twice chosen a censor by the people because of his love for them. The name is intended to draw a parallel in the people's minds.

Pre-occupied with what you rather must do
Than what you should, made you against the grain
To voice him consul. Lay the fault on us.

BRUTUS

Ay, spare us not. Say we read lectures to you,
How youngly he began to serve his country,
How long continued; and what stock he springs of –
The noble house o' th' Marcians; from whence came
That Ancus Marcius, Numa's daughter's son,
Who, after great Hostilius, here was king;
Of the same house Publius and Quintus were,
That our best water brought by conduits hither;
And Censorinus, nobly named so,
Twice being by the people chosen censor,
Was his great ancestor.

SICINIUS

One thus descended,
That hath beside well in his person wrought
To be set high in place, we did commend
To your remembrances; but you have found,
Scaling his present bearing with his past,
That he's your fixed enemy, and revoke
Your sudden approbation.

BRUTUS

Say you ne'er had done't –
Harp on that still – but by our putting on;
And presently, when you have drawn your number
Repair to th' Capitol.

257–8 ***were better . . . greater*** were best risked than for us to wait for a better opportunity.

261 ***vantage*** advantage.

CITIZEN

We will so; almost all
Repent in their election.

Exeunt PLEBEIANS

BRUTUS

Let them go on;
This mutiny were better put in hazard
Than stay, past doubt, for greater.
If, as his nature is, he fall in rage
With their refusal, both observe and answer
The vantage of his anger.

SICINIUS

To th' Capitol, come.
We will be there before the stream o' th' people;
And this shall seem, as partly 'tis, their own,
Which we have goaded onward.

Exeunt

Act 3: summary

The senators are confident that Coriolanus will be elected as consul and so turn to discussing foreign policy as they go to the forum (the market place) for the formal election. They are met by the tribunes who warn them to go no further, saying that the people are incensed at being used so badly and thus are dangerous. The implied threat angers Coriolanus and he turns upon the patricians, accusing them of weakening Rome by giving the people power. He demands that the symbol of this, the post of tribune, be abolished, a demand which leaves him open to a charge of treason under Rome's new constitution. Sicinius and Brutus call the aediles, officers of law, and demand that Coriolanus be arrested. A mob of citizens arrive and the patricians draw their swords: Rome is on the point of civil war.

Coriolanus leads the nobles in driving the citizens off but it is clear that the city is in danger of collapse. He is whisked away by his friends whilst Menenius endeavours to achieve a temporary peace. He agrees to deliver Coriolanus up to the Law.

Volumnia, aware that her son will be sacrificed in order to save Rome, begs him to compromise. He is disgusted by her political expediency, feeling that it is a betrayal of all that she has taught him, and feels isolated from those he holds most dear. However, he allows himself to be schooled into how to play 'the harlot' by his mother, Cominius and Menenius and agrees to placate the mob.

Meanwhile, the tribunes have been coaching the aediles to lead the mob against their enemy. When Coriolanus arrives, he cannot hide his aristocratic scorn of the people and, stung by the accusation of tyranny, lashes out. His outburst confirms the tribunes' declaration that he sees himself as being above the law and results in a sentence of banishment. He contemptuously accepts this, pointing out that it will leave Rome open to attack and cursing them for the tyranny it will bring upon them.

1 ***had made new head*** raised a fresh army.

2–3 ***that it . . . composition*** it was this which caused us to come to terms over Corioli more quickly than we expected to.

Act Three

Scene one

Rome. A street.

Cornets. Enter CORIOLANUS, MENENIUS, *all the Gentry,* COMINIUS, TITUS LARTIUS, *and other* SENATORS.

CORIOLANUS
Tullus Aufidius, then, had made new head?

TITUS LARTIUS
He had, my lord; and that it was which caus'd
Our swifter composition.

CORIOLANUS
So then the Volsces stand but as at first,
Ready, when time shall prompt them, to make road
Upon's again.

COMINIUS
They are worn, Lord Consul, so
That we shall hardly in our ages see
Their banners wave again.

CORIOLANUS
Saw you Aufidius?

TITUS LARTIUS
On safeguard he came to me, and did curse
Against the Volsces, for they had so vilely
Yielded the town. He is retir'd to Antium.

CORIOLANUS
Spoke he of me?

23 ***prank*** flaunt themselves.

24 ***noble sufferance*** what the nobility can bear.

TITUS LARTIUS
He did, my lord.

CORIOLANUS
How? What?

TITUS LARTIUS
How often he had met you, sword to sword;
That of all things upon the earth he hated
Your person most; that he would pawn his fortunes
To hopeless restitution, so he might
Be call'd your vanquisher.

CORIOLANUS
At Antium lives he?

TITUS LARTIUS
At Antium.

CORIOLANUS
I wish I had a cause to seek him there,
To oppose his hatred fully. Welcome home.

Enter SICINIUS *and* BRUTUS.

Behold, these are the tribunes of the people,
The tongues o' th' common mouth. I do despise them,
For they do prank them in authority,
Against all noble sufferance.

SICINIUS
Pass no further.

CORIOLANUS
Ha! What is that?

26 ***It will . . . further*** Brutus warns the nobles against the uprising he has just set into action. The terms in which he puts this are intended to arouse the anger of Coriolanus and so to spur him on to the market place.

30 ***Have I had children's voices?*** Coriolanus refers to the way children change their minds on a whim.

BRUTUS

It will be dangerous to go on – no further.

CORIOLANUS

What makes this change?

MENENIUS

The matter?

COMINIUS

Hath he not pass'd the noble and the common?

BRUTUS

Cominius, no.

CORIOLANUS

Have I had children's voices?

1 SENATOR

Tribunes, give way: he shall to th' market-place.

BRUTUS

The people are incens'd against him.

SICINIUS

Stop,

Or all will fall in broil.

CORIOLANUS

Are these your herd?

Must these have voices, that can yield them now
And straight disclaim their tongues? What are your offices?
You being their mouths, why rule you not their teeth?
Have you not set them on?

43 ***repin'd*** objected.

47 ***sithence*** since then.

MENENIUS

Be calm, be calm.

CORIOLANUS

It is a purpos'd thing, and grows by plot,
To curb the will of the nobility;
Suffer't, and live with such as cannot rule
Nor ever will be rul'd.

BRUTUS

Call't not a plot.
The people cry you mock'd them; and of late,
When corn was given them gratis, you repin'd;
Scandal'd the suppliants for the people, call'd them
Time-pleasers, flatterers, foes to nobleness.

CORIOLANUS

Why, this was known before.

BRUTUS

Not to them all.

CORIOLANUS

Have you inform'd them sithence?

BRUTUS

How? I inform them!

COMINIUS

You are like to do such business.

BRUTUS

Not unlike
Each way to better yours.

CORIOLANUS

Why then should I be consul? By yond clouds,

56–7 ***Or never . . . tribune*** or never be a consul, lacking the nobility to fill the office, nor be paired with Brutus as a tribune.

58 ***palt-ring*** trickery.

66 ***mutable, rank-scented meiny*** changeable, foul-stinking multitude.

Let me deserve so ill as you, and make me
Your fellow tribune.

SICINIUS

You show too much of that
For which the people stir; if you will pass
To where you are bound, you must enquire your
way,
Which you are out of, with a gentler spirit,
Or never be so noble as a consul,
Nor yoke with him for tribune.

MENENIUS

Let's be calm.

COMINIUS

The people are abus'd; set on. This palt-ring
Becomes not Rome; nor has Coriolanus
Deserv'd this so dishonour'd rub, laid falsely
I' th' plain way of his merit.

CORIOLANUS

Tell me of corn!
This was my speech, and I will speak't again –

MENENIUS

Not now, not now.

1 SENATOR

Not in this heat, sir, now.

CORIOLANUS

Now, as I live, I will.
My nobler friends, I crave their pardons.
For the mutable, rank-scented meiny, let them
Regard me as I do not flatter, and

70 ***sedition*** agitation against the rule of law.

77–80 ***so shall . . . them*** so shall I always speak out against diseases which, although they harm us, we go out of our way to catch. Coriolanus is once more not only attacking the people, picturing them as a disease, but also the nobles who have unwisely given them power.

82 ***'Twere well . . . know't*** it was as well that we let the people know of it.

Therein behold themselves. I say again,
In soothing them we nourish 'gainst our Senate
The cockle of rebellion, insolence, sedition,
Which we ourselves have plough'd for, sow'd,
and scatter'd,
By mingling them with us, the honour'd
number,
Who lack not virtue, no, nor power, but that
Which they have given to beggars.

MENENIUS

Well, no more.

1 SENATOR

No more words, we beseech you.

CORIOLANUS

How? no more!
As for my country I have shed my blood,
Not fearing outward force, so shall my lungs
Coin words till their decay against those
measles
Which we disdain should tetter us, yet sought
The very way to catch them.

BRUTUS

You speak o' th' people
As if you were a god, to punish; not
A man of their infirmity.

SICINIUS

'Twere well
We let the people know't.

MENENIUS

What, what? his choler?

89 ***Triton of the minnows*** Triton was a minor sea-god, trumpeter for Neptune. The scorn in the metaphor is thus apparent in its aptness.

90 ***'Twas from the canon*** it was unconstitutional. Cominius is concerned that the tribunes are abusing their office, in that they were meant to reflect public opinion not shape it.

93 ***Hydra*** the many-headed serpent which Hercules killed.

96–7 ***he'll turn your current ... his?*** the metaphor pictures the tribunes diverting the water supply into a ditch and them claiming it as their own. It is intended to warn the patricians against allowing their power, the very life-blood of Rome in his eyes, being ceded to the tribunes.

103–4 ***When, both ... theirs*** Coriolanus, once more using cannibalistic imagery, warns that if the nobility share their power, they will find themselves overpowered.

CORIOLANUS
Choler!
Were I as patient as the midnight sleep,
By Jove, 'twould be my mind!

SICINIUS
It is a mind!
That shall remain a poison where it is,
Not poison any further.

CORIOLANUS
Shall remain!
Hear you this Triton of the minnows? Mark you
His absolute 'shall'?

COMINIUS
'Twas from the canon.

CORIOLANUS
'Shall'!
O good but most unwise patricians! Why,
You grave but reckless senators, have you thus
Given Hydra here to choose an officer
That with his peremptory 'shall', being but
The horn and noise o' th' monster's, wants not
spirit
To say he'll turn your current in a ditch,
And make your channel his? If he have power,
Then vail your ignorance; if none, awake
Your dangerous lenity. If you are learn'd,
Be not as common fools; if you are not,
Let them have cushions by you. You are
plebeians,
If they be senators; and they are no less,
When, both your voices blended, the great'st taste

111–12 ***take ... by th' other*** use one to destroy the other. It is clear from this speech that Coriolanus has concerns beyond his own personal situation and that he genuinely fears for the welfare of Rome.

Most palates theirs. They choose their
magistrate;
And such a one as he, who puts his 'shall',
His popular 'shall', against a graver bench
Than ever frown'd in Greece. By Jove himself,
It makes the consuls base; and my soul aches
To know, when two authorities are up,
Neither supreme, how soon confusion
May enter 'twixt the gap of both and take
The one by th' other.

COMINIUS

Well, on to th' market-place.

CORIOLANUS

Whoever gave that counsel to give forth
The corn o' th' storehouse gratis, as 'twas us'd
Sometime in Greece –

MENENIUS

Well, well, no more of that.

CORIOLANUS

Though there the people had more absolute
pow'r –
I say they nourish'd disobedience, fed
The ruin of the state.

BRUTUS

Why shall the people give
One that speaks thus their voice?

CORIOLANUS

I'll give my reasons,
More worthier than their voices. They know the
corn

129–30 ***could never be ... donation*** could never be the origin of our generous gift.

Was not our recompense, resting well assur'd
They ne'er did service for't; being press'd to th' war
Even when the navel of the state was touch'd,
They would not thread the gates. This kind of service
Did not deserve corn gratis. Being i' th' war,
Their mutinies and revolts, wherein they show'd
Most valour, spoke not for them. Th' accusation
Which they have often made against the Senate,
All cause unborn, could never be the native
Of our so frank donation. Well, what then?
How shall this bosom multiplied digest
The Senate's courtesy? Let deeds express
What's like to be their words: 'We did request it;
We are the greater poll, and in true fear
They gave us our demands'. Thus we debase
The nature of our seats, and make the rabble
Call our cares fears; which will in time
Break ope the locks o' th' Senate and bring in
The crows to peck the eagles.

MENENIUS

Come, enough.

BRUTUS

Enough, with over measure.

CORIOLANUS

No, take more.
What may be sworn by, both divine and human,
Seal what I end withal! This double worship,
Where one part does disdain with cause, the other

148 ***unstable slightness*** irresolution and triviality.

156–7 ***let them ... poison*** Coriolanus here admits that power may seem attractive to the people but warns that it will prove to be deadly to them.

163 ***despite o'erwhelm thee*** contempt overthrow you.

164 ***bald tribunes*** i) literally; ii) lacking intelligence.

Insult without all reason; where gentry, title, wisdom,
Cannot conclude but by the yea and no
Of general ignorance – it must omit
Real necessities, and give way the while
To unstable slightness. Purpose so barr'd, it follows
Nothing is done to purpose. Therefore, beseech you –
You that will be less fearful than discreet;
That love the fundamental part of state
More than you doubt the change on't; that prefer
A noble life before a long, and wish
To jump a body with a dangerous physic
That's sure of death without it – at once pluck out
The multitudinous tongue; let them not lick
The sweet which is their poison. Your dishonour
Mangles true judgment, and bereaves the state
Of that integrity which should become't,
Not having the power to do the good it would,
For th' ill which doth control't.

BRUTUS

Has said enough.

SICINIUS

Has spoken like a traitor and shall answer
As traitors do.

CORIOLANUS

Thou wretch, despite o'erwhelm thee!
What should the people do with these bald tribunes,

167 ***When what's . . . law*** when what is not right cannot be avoided but is made law.

173 ***ædiles*** officers for the tribunes created at the same time they were.

177 ***surety*** stand bail.

On whom depending, their obedience fails
To the greater bench? In a rebellion,
When what's not meet, but what must be, was law,
Then were they chosen; in a better hour
Let what is meet be said it must be meet,
And throw their power i' th' dust.

BRUTUS
Manifest treason!

SICINIUS
This a consul? No.

BRUTUS
The ædiles, ho!

Enter an ÆDILE.

Let him be apprehended.

SICINIUS
Go call the people, (*Exit* ÆDILE) in whose name myself
Attach thee as a traitorous innovator,
A foe to th' public weal. Obey, I charge thee,
And follow to thine answer.

CORIOLANUS
Hence, old goat!

PATRICIANS
We'll surety him.

COMINIUS
Ag'd sir, hands off.

187 The following lines must be thought through carefully before being divided up between the groups on stage. Do they suggest a division between the nobles and citizens or general confusion? Your decision will define who to allocate the shouts for 'Peace!' to, and thus who is seen to be the most constructive party. Is it possible that there are those on each side who seek a peaceful solution just as much as others seek conflict?

CORIOLANUS

Hence, rotten thing! or I shall shake thy bones
Out of thy garments.

SICINIUS

Help, ye citizens!

Enter a rabble of PLEBEIANS, *with the* ÆDILES.

MENENIUS

On both sides more respect.

SICINIUS

Here's he that would take from you all your
power.

BRUTUS

Seize him, ædiles.

PLEBEIANS

Down with him! down with him!

2 SENATOR

Weapons, weapons, weapons!

They all bustle about CORIOLANUS.

ALL

Tribunes! patricians! citizens! What, ho! Sicinius!
Brutus! Coriolanus! Citizens!

PATRICIANS

Peace, peace, peace; stay, hold, peace!

MENENIUS

What is about to be? I am out of breath;
Confusion's near; I cannot speak. You Tribunes
To th' people – Coriolanus, patience!
Speak, good Sicinius.

197 ***This is the way . . . quench*** Menenius pictures the crowd's anger as a fire ready to destroy Rome.

SICINIUS

Hear me, people; peace!

PLEBEIANS

Let's hear our tribune. Peace!
Speak, speak, speak.

SICINIUS

You are at point to lose your liberties.
Marcius would have all from you; Marcius,
Whom late you have nam'd for consul.

MENENIUS

Fie, fie, fie!
This is the way to kindle, not to quench.

1 SENATOR

To unbuild the city, and to lay all flat.

SICINIUS

What is the city but the people?

PLEBEIANS

True,
The people are the city.

BRUTUS

By the consent of all we were establish'd
The people's magistrates.

PLEBEIANS

You so remain.

MENENIUS

And so are like to do.

COMINIUS

That is the way to lay the city flat,

208 ***let us*** it is worth noting the pretensions of the tribunes: here Brutus speaks in a way which could be construed as using the royal 'we'.

To bring the roof to the foundation,
And bury all which yet distinctly ranges
In heaps and piles of ruin.

SICINIUS

This deserves death.

BRUTUS

Or let us stand to our authority
Or let us lose it. We do here pronounce,
Upon the part o' th' people, in whose power
We were elected theirs: Marcius is worthy
Of present death.

SICINIUS

Therefore lay hold of him;
Bear him to th' rock Tarpeian, and from
thence
Into destruction cast him.

BRUTUS

Ædiles, seize him.

PLEBEIANS

Yield, Marcius, yield.

MENENIUS

Hear me one word; beseech you, Tribunes,
Hear me but a word.

ÆDILES

Peace, peace!

MENENIUS

Be that you seem, truly your country's friend,
And temp'rately proceed to what you would
Thus violently redress.

221–3 ***those cold ways . . . violent*** Brutus uses the metaphor of illness to suggest that a violent cure is most suited to a life-threatening disease. His intention is to show that Coriolanus is such a danger to the welfare of Rome that he must be removed from it: any attempt to reform him would merely prolong the potential for destruction he represents.

BRUTUS

Sir, those cold ways,
That seem like prudent helps, are very poisonous
Where the disease is violent. Lay hands upon him
And bear him to the rock.

CORIOLANUS *draws his sword.*

CORIOLANUS

No: I'll die here.
There's some among you have beheld me fighting;
Come, try upon yourselves what you have seen me.

MENENIUS

Down with that sword! Tribunes, withdraw awhile.

BRUTUS

Lay hands upon him.

MENENIUS

Help Marcius, help,
You that be noble; help him, young and old.

PLEBEIANS

Down with him, down with him!

In this mutiny the Tribunes, the ÆDILES, *and the People are beat in.*

MENENIUS

Go, get you to your house; be gone, away.
All will be nought else.

236–7 ***'tis a sore … yourself*** it is a disease in all of us which will not be cured by treating you alone.

2 SENATOR

Get you gone.

CORIOLANUS

Stand fast;
We have as many friends as enemies.

MENENIUS

Shall it be put to that?

1 SENATOR

The gods forbid!
I prithee, noble friend, home to thy house;
Leave us to cure this cause.

MENENIUS

For 'tis a sore upon us
You cannot tent yourself; be gone, beseech you.

COMINIUS

Come, sir, along with us.

CORIOLANUS

I would they were barbarians, as they are,
Though in Rome litter'd not Romans, as they are not,
Though calved i' th' porch o' th' Capitol.

MENENIUS

Be gone.
Put not your worthy rage into your tongue;
One time will owe another.

CORIOLANUS

On fair ground
I could beat forty of them.

247–8 ***And manhood is called . . . fabric*** courage is called stupidity when it stands in the way of a falling building.

249 ***tag*** rabble.

249–51 ***whose rage . . . to bear*** i.e. like flood water they wash away the banks which usually contain them.

MENENIUS

I could myself
Take up a brace o' th' best of them; yea, the two tribunes.

COMINIUS

But now 'tis odds beyond arithmetic,
And manhood is call'd foolery when it stands
Against a falling fabric. Will you hence,
Before the tag return? whose rage doth rend
Like interrupted waters, and o'erbear
What they are us'd to bear.

MENENIUS

Pray you be gone.
I'll try whether my old wit be in request
With those that have but little; this must be patch'd
With cloth of any colour.

COMINIUS

Nay, come away.

Exeunt CORIOLANUS *and* COMINIUS, *with others*

PATRICIAN

This man has marr'd his fortune.

MENENIUS

His nature is too noble for the world:
He would not flatter Neptune for his trident,
Or Jove for's power to thunder. His heart's his mouth;
What his breast forges, that his tongue must vent;
And, being angry, does forget that ever
He heard the name of death.

269 ***Tarpeian rock*** the place on the Capitoline Hill in Rome from where criminals were thrown to their death.

A noise within.

Here's goodly work!

PATRICIAN

I would they were a-bed.

MENENIUS

I would they were in Tiber.
What the vengeance, could he not speak 'em fair?

Re-enter BRUTUS *and* SICINIUS, *with the rabble again.*

SICINIUS

Where is this viper
That would depopulate the city and
Be every man himself?

MENENIUS

You worthy Tribunes –

SICINIUS

He shall be thrown down the Tarpeian rock
With rigorous hands; he hath resisted law,
And therefore law shall scorn him further trial
Than the severity of the public power,
Which he so sets at nought.

1 CITIZEN

He shall well know
The noble tribunes are the people's mouths,
And we their hands.

PLEBEIANS

He shall, sure on't.

277–8 ***Do not cry . . . warrant*** in another hunting metaphor, Menenius upbraids the tribunes for inciting more violence when they should be acting appropriately.

MENENIUS

Sir, sir –

SICINIUS

Peace!

MENENIUS

Do not cry havoc, where you should but hunt
With modest warrant.

SICINIUS

Sir, how comes't that you
Have holp to make this rescue?

MENENIUS

Hear me speak.
As I do know the consul's worthiness,
So can I name his faults.

SICINIUS

Consul! What consul?

MENENIUS

The consul Coriolanus.

BRUTUS

He consul!

PLEBEIANS

No, no, no, no, no.

MENENIUS

If, by the tribune's leave, and yours, good people,
I may be heard, I would crave a word or two;
The which shall turn you to no further harm
Than so much loss of time.

288 ***peremptory*** resolute.

295 ***unnatural dam*** unnatural mother. Rome was frequently pictured as a mother as in its mythological origin, its founders were suckled by she-wolves, giving them courage and fortitude.

306 ***kam*** perverse.

SICINIUS

Speak briefly, then,
For we are peremptory to dispatch
This viperous traitor; to eject him hence
Were but one danger, and to keep him here
Our certain death; therefore it is decreed
He dies to-night.

MENENIUS

Now the good gods forbid
That our renowned Rome, whose gratitude
Towards her deserved children is enroll'd
In Jove's own book, like an unnatural dam
Should now eat up her own!

SICINIUS

He's a disease that must be cut away.

MENENIUS

O, he's a limb that has but a disease –
Mortal, to cut it off: to cure it, easy.
What has he done to Rome that's worthy death?
Killing our enemies, the blood he hath lost –
Which I dare vouch is more than that he hath
By many an ounce – he dropt it for his country;
And what is left, to lose it by his country
Were to us all that do't and suffer it
A brand to th' end o' th' world.

SICINIUS

This is clean kam.

BRUTUS

Merely awry. When he did love his country,
It honour'd him.

314–16 ***This tiger-footed ... heels*** this swift acting rage, when it shall have time to see the harm done by its thoughtless haste, will, too late, move at a more considered pace.

SICINIUS

The service of the foot,
Being once gangren'd, is not then respected
For what before it was.

BRUTUS

We'll hear no more.
Pursue him to his house and pluck him thence,
Lest his infection, being of catching nature,
Spread further.

MENENIUS

One word more, one word!
This tiger-footed rage, when it shall find
The harm of unscann'd swiftness, will, too late,
Tie leaden pounds to's heels. Proceed by process,
Lest parties – as he is belov'd – break out,
And sack great Rome with Romans.

BRUTUS

If it were so –

SICINIUS

What do ye talk?
Have we not had a taste of his obedience –
Our ædiles smote, ourselves resisted? Come!

MENENIUS

Consider this: he has been bred i' th' wars
Since 'a could draw a sword, and is ill school'd
In bolted language; meal and bran together
He throws without distinction. Give me leave,
I'll go to him and undertake to bring him
Where he shall answer by a lawful form,
In peace, to his utmost peril.

328 ***Noble Tribunes*** the title, intended to flatter, is deeply ironic.

1 SENATOR

Noble Tribunes,
It is the humane way; the other course
Will prove too bloody, and the end of it
Unknown to the beginning.

SICINIUS

Noble Menenius,
Be you then as the people's officer.
Masters, lay down your weapons.

BRUTUS

Go not home.

SICINIUS

Meet on the market-place. We'll attend you
there;
Where, if you bring not Marcius, we'll proceed
In our first way.

MENENIUS

I'll bring him to you.
(*To the* SENATORS) Let me desire your company;
he must come,
Or what is worst will follow.

1 SENATOR

Pray you let's to him.

Exeunt

9–10 ***To call them . . . groats*** to call them slaves, things created to be bought and sold for little money.

Scene two

Rome. The house of Coriolanus.

Enter CORIOLANUS *with* NOBLES.

CORIOLANUS

Let them pull all about mine ears, present me
Death on the wheel or at wild horses' heels;
Or pile ten hills on the Tarpeian rock,
That the precipitation might down stretch
Below the beam of sight; yet will I still
Be thus to them.

1 PATRICIAN

You do the nobler.

CORIOLANUS

I muse my mother
Does not approve me further, who was wont
To call them woollen vassals, things created
To buy and sell with groats; to show bare heads
In congregations, to yawn, be still, and wonder,
When one but of my ordinance stood up
To speak of peace or war.

Enter VOLUMNIA.

I talk of you:
Why did you wish me milder? Would you have me
False to my nature? Rather say I play
The man I am.

VOLUMNIA

O, sir, sir, sir,
I would have had you put your power well on
Before you had worn it out.

21 ***thwartings of your dispositions*** frustrating your desires.

CORIOLANUS

Let go.

VOLUMNIA

You might have been enough the man you are
With striving less to be so; lesser had been
The thwartings of your dispositions, if
You had not show'd them how ye were dispos'd,
Ere they lack'd power to cross you.

CORIOLANUS

Let them hang.

VOLUMNIA

Ay, and burn too.

Enter MENENIUS *with the* SENATORS.

MENENIUS

Come, come, you have been too rough,
something too rough;
You must return and mend it.

1 SENATOR

There's no remedy,
Unless, by not so doing, our good city
Cleave in the midst and perish.

VOLUMNIA

Pray be counsell'd;
I have a heart as little apt as yours,
But yet a brain that leads my use of anger
To better vantage.

MENENIUS

Well said, noble woman!
Before he should thus stoop to th' herd, but that

33 ***physic*** medicine.

41 ***extremities speak*** absolute necessities demand.

42 ***unsever'd*** inseparable.

The violent fit o' th' time craves it as physic
For the whole state, I would put mine armour on,
Which I can scarcely bear.

CORIOLANUS

What must I do?

MENENIUS

Return to th' tribunes.

CORIOLANUS

Well, what then, what then?

MENENIUS

Repent what you have spoke.

CORIOLANUS

For them! I cannot do it to the gods;
Must I then do't to them?

VOLUMNIA

You are too absolute;
Though therein you can never be too noble
But when extremities speak. I have heard you say
Honour and policy, like unsever'd friends,
I' th' war do grow together; grant that, and tell me
In peace what each of them by th' other lose
That they combine not there.

CORIOLANUS

Tush, tush!

MENENIUS

A good demand.

55–6 ***roted ... tongue*** learnt off by heart, i.e. which you do not need to mean.

60–1 ***Which else ... blood*** she likens the action of speaking kindly to the people to taking a town by diplomacy rather than having to attack it. (It is telling that both actions result in people being enslaved.)

VOLUMNIA

If it be honour in your wars to seem
The same you are not, which for your best ends
You adopt your policy, how is it less or worse
That it shall hold companionship in peace
With honour as in war; since that to both
It stands in like request?

CORIOLANUS

Why force you this?

VOLUMNIA

Because that now it lies you on to speak
To th' people, not by your own instruction,
Nor by th' matter which your heart prompts you,
But with such words that are but roted in
Your tongue, though but bastards and syllables
Of no allowance to your bosom's truth.
Now, this no more dishonours you at all
Than to take in a town with gentle words,
Which else would put you to your fortune and
The hazard of much blood.
I would dissemble with my nature where
My fortunes and my friends at stake requir'd
I should do so in honour. I am in this
Your wife, your son, these senators, the nobles;
And you will rather show our general louts
How you can frown, than spend a fawn upon 'em
For the inheritance of their loves and safeguard
Of what that want might ruin.

MENENIUS

Noble lady!
Come, go with us, speak fair; you may salve so,

75 ***bussing*** kissing.

79–80 ***Now humble . . . handling!*** the mulberry was commonly used as an image of readiness to yield. Its application to Coriolanus seems ridiculous and indicates how seriously Volumnia holds the action of supplicating to the crowd: for her, it is merely a means to an end.

88 ***they have pardons*** i.e. the power to pardon.

Not what is dangerous present, but the loss
Of what is past.

VOLUMNIA

I prithee now, my son,
Go to them with this bonnet in thy hand;
And thus far having stretch'd it – here be with them –
Thy knee bussing the stones – for in such business
Action is eloquence, and the eyes of th' ignorant
More learned than the ears – waving thy head,
Which often thus correcting thy stout heart,
Now humble as the ripest mulberry
That will not hold the handling. Or say to them
Thou art their soldier and, being bred in broils,
Hast not the soft way which, thou dost confess,
Were fit for thee to use, as they to claim,
In asking their good loves; but thou wilt frame
Thyself, forsooth, hereafter theirs, so far
As thou hast power and person.

MENENIUS

This but done
Even as she speaks, why, their hearts were yours;
For they have pardons, being ask'd, as free
As words to little purpose.

VOLUMNIA

Prithee now,
Go, and be rul'd; although I know thou hadst rather
Follow thine enemy in a fiery gulf
Than flatter him in a bower.

99 ***unbarb'd sconce*** uncovered head.

Enter COMINIUS.

Here is Cominius.

COMINIUS

I have been i' th' market-place; and, sir, 'tis fit
You make strong party, or defend yourself
By calmness or by absence; all's in anger.

MENENIUS

Only fair speech.

COMINIUS

I think 'twill serve, if he
Can thereto frame his spirit.

VOLUMNIA

He must and will.
Prithee now, say you will, and go about it.

CORIOLANUS

Must I go show them my unbarb'd sconce?
Must I
With my base tongue give to my noble heart
A lie that it must bear? Well, I will do't;
Yet, were there but this single plot to lose,
This mould of Marcius, they to dust should grind
it,
And throw't against the wind. To th' market-place!
You have put me now to such a part which never
I shall discharge to th' life.

COMINIUS

Come, come, we'll prompt you.

VOLUMNIA

I prithee now, sweet son, as thou hast said

120–23 ***I will not . . . baseness*** Coriolanus fears that by undertaking such a hypocritical action he will corrupt his mind permanently.

My praises made thee first a soldier, so,
To have my praise for this, perform a part
Thou hast not done before.

CORIOLANUS

Well, I must do't.
Away, my disposition, and possess me
Some harlot's spirit! My throat of war be turn'd,
Which quier'd with my drum, into a pipe
Small as an eunuch or the virgin voice
That babies lulls asleep! The smiles of knaves
Tent in my cheeks, and schoolboys' tears take up
The glasses of my sight! A beggar's tongue
Make motion through my lips, and my arm'd knees,
Who bow'd but in my stirrup, bend like his
That hath receiv'd an alms! I will not do't,
Lest I surcease to honour mine own truth,
And by my body's action teach my mind
A most inherent baseness.

VOLUMNIA

At thy choice, then.
To beg of thee, it is my more dishonour
Than thou of them. Come all to ruin. Let
Thy mother rather feel thy pride than fear
Thy dangerous stoutness; for I mock at death
With as big heart as thou. Do as thou list.
Thy valiantness was mine, thou suck'dst it from me;
But owe thy pride thyself.

132 ***mountebank their loves*** mountebanks were quacks who sold fake cures from platforms in town squares. They were, thus, conmen who relied upon their patter to make money.

133 ***Cog*** swindle.

137 ***Do your will*** Volumnia's curt dismissal could be caused by the way he has mocked her protestations that to pretend love for the people would be a noble thing to do. He has said that it is nothing more than a common swindler's trick.

CORIOLANUS

Pray be content.
Mother, I am going to the market-place;
Chide me no more. I'll mountebank their loves,
Cog their hearts from them, and come home belov'd
Of all the trades in Rome. Look, I am going.
Commend me to my wife. I'll return consul,
Or never trust to what my tongue can do
I' th' way of flattery further.

VOLUMNIA

Do your will.

Exit

COMINIUS

Away! The tribunes do attend you. Arm yourself
To answer mildly; for they are prepar'd
With accusations, as I hear, more strong
Than are upon you yet.

CORIOLANUS

The word is 'mildly'. Pray you let us go.
Let them accuse me by invention; I
Will answer in mine honour.

MENENIUS

Ay, but mildly.

CORIOLANUS

Well, mildly be it then – mildly.

Exeunt

3 ***Enforce*** attack.

Scene three

Rome. The Forum.

Enter SICINIUS *and* BRUTUS.

BRUTUS

In this point charge him home, that he affects
Tyrannical power. If he evade us there,
Enforce him with his envy to the people,
And that the spoil got on the Antiates
Was ne'er distributed.

Enter an ÆDILE.

What, will he come?

ÆDILE

He's coming.

BRUTUS

How accompanied?

ÆDILE

With old Menenius, and those senators
That always favour'd him.

SICINIUS

Have you a catalogue
Of all the voices that we have procur'd,
Set down by th' poll?

ÆDILE

I have; 'tis ready.

SICINIUS

Have you collected them by tribes?

15 ***For death . . . or banishment*** the possible punishments Coriolanus faces for treason. Notice how the whole event is to be stage managed by the tribunes.

18 ***And power . . . cause*** in the justice of the cause. The rhetorical flourish suggests that he is enjoying his new power.

ÆDILE

I have.

SICINIUS

Assemble presently the people hither;
And when they hear me say 'It shall be so
I' th' right and strength o' th' commons' be it either
For death, for fine, or banishment, then let them,
If I say fine, cry 'Fine!' – if death, cry 'Death!'
Insisting on the old prerogative
And power i' th' truth o' th' cause.

ÆDILE

I shall inform them.

BRUTUS

And when such time they have begun to cry,
Let them not cease, but with a din confus'd
Enforce the present execution
Of what we chance to sentence.

ÆDILE

Very well.

SICINIUS

Make them be strong, and ready for this hint,
When we shall hap to give't them.

BRUTUS

Go about it.

Exit ÆDILE

Put him to choler straight. He hath been us'd
Ever to conquer, and to have his worth

27–8 ***being once chaf'd ... temperance*** being once aroused, he cannot be calmed down.

29–30 ***that is there ... neck*** there is enough in that, with a little help from us, to have him thrown from the Tarpeian rock.

32–3 ***as an ostler ... volume*** as an ostler will, for the smallest sum of money, put up with being called a knave repeatedly.

Of contradiction; being once chaf'd, he cannot
Be rein'd again to temperance; then he speaks
What's in his heart, and that is there which
looks
With us to break his neck.

Enter CORIOLANUS, MENENIUS, *and* COMINIUS, *with others.*

SICINIUS

Well, here he comes.

MENENIUS

Calmly, I do beseech you.

CORIOLANUS

Ay, as an ostler, that for th' poorest piece
Will bear the knave by th' volume. Th' honour'd
gods
Keep Rome in safety, and the chairs of justice
Supplied with worthy men! plant love among's!
Throng our large temples with the shows of
peace,
And not our streets with war!

1 SENATOR

Amen, amen!

MENENIUS

A noble wish.

Re-enter the ÆDILE, *with the* PLEBEIANS.

SICINIUS

Draw near, ye people.

ÆDILE

List to your tribunes. Audience! peace, I say!

43 ***demand*** i.e. demand to know.

45 ***Allow*** acknowledge.

CORIOLANUS
First, hear me speak.

BOTH TRIBUNES
Well, say. Peace, ho!

CORIOLANUS
Shall I be charg'd no further than this present?
Must all determine here?

SICINIUS
I do demand,
If you submit you to the people's voices,
Allow their officers, and are content
To suffer lawful censure for such faults
As shall be prov'd upon you.

CORIOLANUS
I am content.

MENENIUS
Lo, citizens, he says he is content.
The warlike service he has done, consider; think
Upon the wounds his body bears, which show
Like graves i' th' holy churchyard.

CORIOLANUS
Scratches with briers,
Scars to move laughter only.

MENENIUS
Consider further,
That when he speaks not like a citizen,
You find him like a soldier; do not take
His rougher accents for malicious sounds,
But, as I say, such as become a soldier
Rather than envy you.

65 ***a power tyrranical*** aiming to be king.

COMINIUS

Well, well! No more.

CORIOLANUS

What is the matter,
That being pass'd for consul with full voice,
I am so dishonour'd that the very hour
You take it off again?

SICINIUS

Answer to us.

CORIOLANUS

Say then; 'tis true, I ought so.

SICINIUS

We charge you that you have contriv'd to take
From Rome all season'd office, and to wind
Yourself into a power tyrannical;
For which you are a traitor to the people.

CORIOLANUS

How – traitor?

MENENIUS

Nay, temperately! Your promise.

CORIOLANUS

The fires i' th' lowest hell fold in the people!
Call me their traitor! Thou injurious tribune!
Within thine eyes sat twenty thousand deaths
In thy hands clutch'd as many millions, in
Thy lying tongue both numbers, I would say
'Thou liest' unto thee with a voice as free
As I do pray the gods.

81 ***Opposing laws with strokes*** using force to oppose legal proceedings.

83 ***capital kind*** i.e. punishable by death.

SICINIUS

Mark you this, people?

PLEBEIANS

To th' rock, to th' rock, with him!

SICINIUS

Peace!
We need not put new matter to his charge.
What you have seen him do and heard him
speak,
Beating your officers, cursing yourselves,
Opposing laws with strokes, and here defying
Those whose great power must try him – even
this,
So criminal and in such capital kind,
Deserves th' extremest death.

BRUTUS

But since he hath
Serv'd well for Rome –

CORIOLANUS

What do you prate of service?

BRUTUS

I talk of that that know it.

CORIOLANUS

You!

MENENIUS

Is this the promise that you made your mother?

COMINIUS

Know, I pray you –

99 ***not*** not only.

104 ***In peril of precipitation*** in danger of being thrown off.

CORIOLANUS

I'll know no further.
Let them pronounce the steep Tarpeian death,
Vagabond exile, flaying, pent to linger
But with a grain a day, I would not buy
Their mercy at the price of one fair word,
Nor check my courage for what they can give,
To have't with saying 'Good morrow'.

SICINIUS

For that he has –
As much as in him lies – from time to time
Envied against the people, seeking means
To pluck away their power; as now at last
Given hostile strokes, and that not in the presence
Of dreaded justice, but on the ministers
That do distribute it – in the name o' th' people,
And in the power of us the tribunes, we,
Ev'n from this instant, banish him our city,
In peril of precipitation
From off the rock Tarpeian, never more
To enter our Rome gates. I' th' people's name,
I say it shall be so.

PLEBEIANS

It shall be so, it shall be so! Let him away!
He's banish'd, and it shall be so.

COMINIUS

Hear me, my masters and my common friends –

SICINIUS

He's sentenc'd; no more hearing.

131–5 ***Your ignorance … blows!*** your ignorance, which prevents you from seeing things until they affect you, will lead to your expelling all of your protectors. Thus it will make you vulnerable to a foreign power, which will overcome you without blows. In this he ironically foresees the ruin he will bring to his home.

142 ***vexation*** abuse.

COMINIUS

Let me speak.
I have been consul, and can show for Rome
Her enemies' marks upon me. I do love
My country's good with a respect more tender,
More holy and profound, than mine own life,
My dear wife's estimate, her womb's increase
And treasure of my loins. Then if I would
Speak that –

SICINIUS

We know your drift. Speak what?

BRUTUS

There's no more to be said, but he is banish'd,
As enemy to the people and his country.
It shall be so.

PLEBEIANS

It shall be so, it shall be so.

CORIOLANUS

You common cry of curs, whose breath I hate
As reek o' th' rotten fens, whose loves I prize
As the dead carcasses of unburied men
That do corrupt my air – I banish you.
And here remain with your uncertainty!
Let every feeble rumour shake your hearts;
Your enemies, with nodding of their plumes,
Fan you into despair! Have the power still
To banish your defenders, till at length
Your ignorance – which finds not till it feels,
Making but reservation of yourselves
Still your own foes – deliver you
As most abated captives to some nation

135–6 ***Despising . . . city*** despising the city because of your presence in it.

142 ***vexation*** abuse.

That won you without blows! Despising
For you the city, thus I turn my back;
There is a world elsewhere.

Exeunt CORIOLANUS, COMINIUS, MENENIUS, *with the other* PATRICIANS

ÆDILE
The people's enemy is gone, is gone!

They all shout and throw up their caps.

PLEBEIANS
Our enemy is banish'd, he is gone! Hoo-oo!

SICINIUS
Go see him out at gates, and follow him,
As he hath follow'd you, with all despite;
Give him deserv'd vexation. Let a guard
Attend us through the city.

PLEBEIANS
Come, come, let's see him out at gates; come!
The gods preserve our noble tribunes! Come.

Exeunt

Act 4: summary

Coriolanus finds that now all that he has lived for, to serve Rome, is meaningless and so he must forge a new existence for himself. He sets out into an unknown world, picturing himself as a 'lonely dragon'. He rejects Cominius' offer of companionship and refuses to allow anyone to accompany him beyond the city gates. Rome is now at peace, yet the fragility of this can be seen by an early clash between the tribunes and Volumnia. The city's vunerability is shown in the meeting of a Volscian and a Roman traitor, who passes on the news of the banishment of Coriolanus to the enemy.

Lacking a mission, Coriolanus is drawn to Antium, and, particularly, to the home of Aufidius. Throwing himself at the mercy of his former foe, he expresses a desire to create a new identity as an enemy to Rome. He offers himself up to Aufidius, who pledges a love greater than their former enmity. Together they will wage war once more.

In Rome, the tribunes taunt a cowed Menenius with the lack of impact that Coriolanus' exile has had on the city. Their picture of domestic harmony is interrupted by a report of the incipient attack, which they dismiss as lies. However, they cannot dismiss Cominius' account of events in Antium and are thrown into panic by Menenius' belief that Coriolanus will show little mercy to the city which has betrayed him. They are now the ones who are scorned for their 'good work' which has left Rome open to attack. As expected, the citizens fly into panic at the news.

Aufidius, in conversation with a lieutenant, shows himself to have been by no means sincere in his protestations of love to Coriolanus. He is angered by the way the latter has carried out his new commission, throwing him into the shade, and once more pledges to be avenged. Although unclear as to how this will be achieved, he predicts that when Coriolanus has destroyed his native city, then he will be at his most vunerable.

7–9 ***fortune's blows . . . cunning*** when fate strikes cruelly, it is a sign of nobility to be able to take one's misfortune calmly.

13 ***red pestilence*** typhus.

Act Four

Scene one

Rome. Before a gate of the city.

Enter CORIOLANUS, VOLUMNIA, VIRGILIA, MENENIUS, COMINIUS, *with the young nobility of Rome.*

CORIOLANUS

Come, leave your tears; a brief farewell. The beast
With many heads butts me away. Nay, mother,
Where is your ancient courage? You were us'd
To say extremities was the trier of spirits;
That common chances common men could bear;
That when the sea was calm all boats alike
Show'd mastership in floating; fortune's blows,
When most struck home, being gentle wounded craves
A noble cunning. You were us'd to load me
With precepts that would make invincible
The heart that conn'd them.

VIRGILIA

O heavens! O heavens!

CORIOLANUS

Nay, I prithee, woman –

VOLUMNIA

Now the red pestilence strike all trades in Rome,
And occupations perish!

17 ***Hercules*** a Greek demi-god who was given twelve tasks to perform.

26–7 ***'Tis fond … at 'em*** it is as foolish to cry out at the inevitable as it is to laugh at it.

31–3 ***your son … practice*** your son will do something exceptional or be caught by crafty deceits or trickery. The statement will prove to be cruelly prophetic.

36–7 ***More than … thee*** more than exposing yourself to whatever fate can throw in your way.

CORIOLANUS

What, what, what!
I shall be lov'd when I am lack'd. Nay, mother,
Resume that spirit when you were wont to say,
If you had been the wife of Hercules,
Six of his labours you'd have done, and sav'd
Your husband so much sweat. Cominius,
Droop not; adieu. Farewell, my wife, my mother.
I'll do well yet. Thou old and true Menenius,
Thy tears are salter than a younger man's
And venomous to thine eyes. My sometime General,
I have seen thee stern, and thou hast oft beheld
Heart-hard'ning spectacles; tell these sad women
'Tis fond to wail inevitable strokes,
As 'tis to laugh at 'em. My mother, you wot well
My hazards still have been your solace; and
Believe't not lightly – though I go alone,
Like to a lonely dragon, that his fen
Makes fear'd and talk'd of more than seen – your son
Will or exceed the common or be caught
With cautelous baits and practice.

VOLUMNIA

My first son,
Whither wilt thou go? Take good Cominius
With thee awhile; determine on some course
More than a wild exposture to each chance
That starts i' th' way before thee.

VIRGILIA

O the gods!

43 ***advantage*** the opportunity.

52–3 ***never . . . me formerly*** the line will gain irony from his later defection to the Volscians. However, in some respects, it will prove to be correct, in that his unbending pride, cause of his banishment here, will lead to his death.

COMINIUS

I'll follow thee a month, devise with thee
Where thou shalt rest, that thou mayst hear of us,
And we of thee; so, if the time thrust forth
A cause for thy repeal, we shall not send
O'er the vast world to seek a single man,
And lose advantage, which doth ever cool
I' th' absence of the needer.

CORIOLANUS

Fare ye well;
Thou hast years upon thee, and thou art too full
Of the wars' surfeits to go rove with one
That's yet unbruis'd; bring me but out at gate.
Come, my sweet wife, my dearest mother, and
My friends of noble touch; when I am forth,
Bid me farewell, and smile. I pray you come.
While I remain above the ground you shall
Hear from me still, and never of me aught
But what is like me formerly.

MENENIUS

That's worthily
As any ear can hear. Come, let's not weep.
If I could shake off but one seven years
From these old arms and legs, by the good gods,
I'd with thee every foot.

CORIOLANUS

Give me thy hand.
Come.

Exeunt

1 ***'we'll no further'*** i.e. 'there is nothing more to be gained by this show of power.' The tribunes show themselves to be keenly aware of when to use their power and when to hide it.

Scene two

Rome. A street near the gate.

Enter the two TRIBUNES, SICINIUS *and* BRUTUS, *with the* ÆDILE.

SICINIUS

Bid them all home; he's gone, and we'll no
further.
The nobility are vex'd, whom we see have sided
In his behalf.

BRUTUS

Now we have shown our power,
Let us seem humbler after it is done
Than when it was a-doing.

SICINIUS

Bid them home.
Say their great enemy is gone, and they
Stand in their ancient strength.

BRUTUS

Dismiss them home.

Exit ÆDILE

Here comes his mother.

Enter VOLUMNIA, VIRGILIA, *and* MENENIUS.

SICINIUS

Let's not meet her.

BRUTUS

Why?

SICINIUS

They say she's mad.

11 ***hoarded*** i.e. which the gods hoard up to punish mortals with.

BRUTUS

They have ta'en note of us; keep on your way.

VOLUMNIA

O, y'are well met; th' hoarded plague o' th' gods
Requite your love!

MENENIUS

Peace, peace, be not so loud.

VOLUMNIA

If that I could for weeping, you should hear –
Nay, and you shall hear some. (*To* BRUTUS) Will
you be gone?

VIRGILIA

(*To* SICINIUS) You shall stay too. I would I had the
power
To say so to my husband.

SICINIUS

Are you mankind?

VOLUMNIA

Ay, fool; is that a shame? Note but this, fool:
Was not a man my father? Hadst thou foxship
To banish him that struck more blows for Rome
Than thou hast spoken words?

SICINIUS

O blessed heavens!

VOLUMNIA

Moe noble blows than ever thou wise words;
And for Rome's good. I'll tell thee what – yet go!
Nay, but thou shalt stay too. I would my son
Were in Arabia, and thy tribe before him,
His good sword in his hand.

26 ***He'd make … posterity*** he'd finish off your race.

SICINIUS

What then?

VIRGILIA

What then!

He'd make an end of thy posterity.

VOLUMNIA

Bastards and all.
Good man, the wounds that he does bear for Rome!

MENENIUS

Come, come, peace.

SICINIUS

I would he had continued to his country
As he began, and not unknit himself
The noble knot he made.

BRUTUS

I would he had.

VOLUMNIA

'I would he had'! 'Twas you incens'd the rabble –
Cats that can judge as fitly of his worth
As I can of those mysteries which heaven
Will not have earth to know.

BRUTUS

Pray, let's go.

VOLUMNIA

Now, pray, sir, get you gone;
You have done a brave deed. Ere you go, hear this:
As far as doth the Capitol exceed
The meanest house in Rome, so far my son –

52–3 ***Leave this . . . Juno-like*** stop this pathetic whimpering, as I have done, and leave with the stateliness of a queen. There is an unintentional irony here as Juno, in anger, caused the destruction of the Trojans, the ancestors of the Romans. By perpetuating the civil strife, Volumnia risks bringing the same fate to Rome.

This lady's husband here, this, do you see? –
Whom you have banish'd does exceed you all.

BRUTUS

Well, well, we'll leave you.

SICINIUS

Why stay we to be baited
With one that wants her wits?

Exeunt TRIBUNES

VOLUMNIA

Take my prayers with you.
I would the gods had nothing else to do
But to confirm my curses. Could I meet 'em
But once a day, it would unclog my heart
Of what lies heavy to't.

MENENIUS

You have told them home,
And, by my troth, you have cause. You'll sup with me?

VOLUMNIA

Anger's my meat; I sup upon myself,
And so shall starve with feeding. Come, let's go.
Leave this faint puling and lament as I do,
In anger, Juno-like. Come, come, come.

Exeunt VOLUMNIA *and* VIRGILIA

MENENIUS

Fie, fie, fie!

Exit

4–5 ***my services . . . against 'em*** like you, I am an enemy of Rome.

9 ***favour . . . tongue*** I recognise you now that I have heard you speak.

Scene three

A highway between Rome and Antium.

Enter a ROMAN *and a* VOLSCE, *meeting.*

ROMAN

I know you well, sir, and you know me; your name, I think, is Adrian.

VOLSCE

It is so, sir. Truly, I have forgot you.

ROMAN

I am a Roman; and my services are, as you are, against 'em. Know you me yet?

VOLSCE

Nicanor? No!

ROMAN

The same, sir.

VOLSCE

You had more beard when I last saw you, but your favour is well appear'd by your tongue. What's the news in Rome? I have a note from the Volscian state, to find you out there. You have well saved me a day's journey.

ROMAN

There hath been in Rome strange insurrections: the people against the senators, patricians, and nobles.

VOLSCE

Hath been! Is it ended, then? Our state thinks not so; they are in a most warlike preparation,

38 ***He cannot choose*** he cannot fail to.

and hope to come upon them in the heat of their division.

ROMAN

The main blaze of it is past, but a small thing would make it flame again; for the nobles receive so to heart the banishment of that worthy Coriolanus that they are in a ripe aptness to take all power from the people, and to pluck from them their tribunes for ever. This lies glowing, I can tell you, and is almost mature for the violent breaking out.

VOLSCE

Coriolanus banish'd!

ROMAN

Banish'd, sir.

VOLSCE

You will be welcome with this intelligence, Nicanor.

ROMAN

The day serves well for them now. I have heard it said the fittest time to corrupt a man's wife is when she's fall'n out with her husband. Your noble Tullus Aufidius will appear well in these wars, his great opposer, Coriolanus, being now in no request of his country.

VOLSCE

He cannot choose. I am most fortunate thus accidentally to encounter you; you have ended my business, and I will merrily accompany you home.

47 ***distinctly billeted*** separately enrolled.

3 ***fore my wars*** in the face of my onslaught.

ROMAN

I shall between this and supper tell you most strange things from Rome, all tending to the good of their adversaries. Have you an army ready, say you?

VOLSCE

A most royal one: the centurions and their charges, distinctly billeted, already in th' entertainment, and to be on foot at an hour's warning.

ROMAN

I am joyful to hear of their readiness, and am the man, I think, that shall set them in present action. So, sir, heartily well met, and most glad of your company.

VOLSCE

You take my part from me, sir. I have the most cause to be glad of yours.

ROMAN

Well, let us go together.

Exeunt

Scene four

Antium. Before Aufidius's house.

Enter CORIOLANUS *in mean apparel, disguised and muffled.*

CORIOLANUS

A goodly city is this Antium. City,
'Tis I that made thy widows; many an heir
Of these fair edifices fore my wars

12 ***slippery turns*** unpredictable changes.

15 ***still*** always.

Have I heard groan and drop. Then know me not,
Lest that thy wives with spits and boys with stones,
In puny battle slay me.

Enter a CITIZEN.

Save you, sir.

CITIZEN

And you.

CORIOLANUS

Direct me, if it be your will,
Where great Aufidius lies. Is he in Antium?

CTIZEN

He is, and feasts the nobles of the state
At his house this night.

CORIOLANUS

Which is his house, beseech you?

CITIZEN

This here before you.

CORIOLANUS

Thank you, sir; farewell.

Exit CITIZEN

O world, thy slippery turns! Friends now fast sworn,
Whose double bosoms seems to wear one heart,
Whose hours, whose bed, whose meal and exercise
Are still together, who twin, as 'twere, in love

21 ***trick not worth an egg*** a worthless trifle.

Unseparable, shall within this hour,
On a dissension of a doit, break out
To bitterest enmity; so fellest foes,
Whose passions and whose plots have broke their sleep
To take the one the other, by some chance,
Some trick not worth an egg, shall grow dear friends
And interjoin their issues. So with me:
My birthplace hate I, and my love's upon
This enemy town. I'll enter. If he slay me,
He does fair justice; if he give me way,
I'll do his country service.

Exit

Scene five

Antium. Aufidius's house.

Music plays. Enter a SERVINGMAN.

1 SERVINGMAN
Wine, wine, wine! What service is here! I think our fellows are asleep.

Exit

Enter another SERVINGMAN.

2 SERVINGMAN
Where's Cotus? My master calls for him. Cotus!

Exit

Enter CORIOLANUS.

8–9 ***I have . . . Coriolanus*** this is said as an aside.

CORIOLANUS

A goodly house. The feast smells well, but I
Appear not like a guest.

Re-enter the first SERVINGMAN.

1 SERVINGMAN

What would you have, friend? Whence are you?
Here's no place for you: pray go to the door.

Exit

CORIOLANUS

I have deserv'd no better entertainment
In being Coriolanus.

Re-enter second SERVINGMAN.

2 SERVINGMAN

Whence are you, sir? Has the porter his eyes in his head that he gives entrance to such companions? Pray get you out.

CORIOLANUS

Away!

2 SERVINGMAN

Away? Get you away.

CORIOLANUS

Now th' art troublesome.

2 SERVINGMAN

Are you so brave? I'll have you talk'd with anon.

Enter a third SERVINGMAN. *The first meets him.*

3 SERVINGMAN

What fellow's this?

31 ***go and batten on cold bits*** go and gorge yourself on scraps of left-over meat.

1 SERVINGMAN

A strange one as ever I look'd on. I cannot get him out o' th' house. Prithee call my master to him.

3 SERVINGMAN

What have you to do here, fellow? Pray you avoid the house.

CORIOLANUS

Let me but stand – I will not hurt your hearth.

3 SERVINGMAN

What are you?

CORIOLANUS

A gentleman.

3 SERVINGMAN

A marv'llous poor one.

CORIOLANUS

True, so I am.

3 SERVINGMAN

Pray you, poor gentleman, take up some other station; here's no place for you. Pray you avoid. Come.

CORIOLANUS

Follow your function, go and batten on cold bits. (*Pushes him away from him.*)

3 SERVINGMAN

What, you will not? Prithee tell my master what a strange guest he has here.

37 ***Under the canopy*** under the sky.

41 ***I' th' city of kites and crows*** both these birds are associated with battles, feeding as they do on corpses.

46–7 ***'Tis an honester . . . mistress*** i.e. to commit adultery.

48 ***trencher*** serving tray.

2 SERVINGMAN
And I shall.

Exit

3 SERVINGMAN
Where dwell'st thou?

CORIOLANUS
Under the canopy.

3 SERVINGMAN
Under the canopy?

CORIOLANUS
Ay.

3 SERVINGMAN
Where's that?

CORIOLANUS
I' th' city of kites and crows.

3 SERVINGMAN
I' th' city of kites and crows! What an ass it is! Then thou dwell'st with daws too?

CORIOLANUS
No, I serve not thy master.

3 SERVINGMAN
How, sir! Do you meddle with my master?

CORIOLANUS
Ay; 'tis an honester service than to meddle with thy mistress. Thou prat'st and prat'st; serve with thy trencher; hence! (*Beats him away.*)

Enter AUFIDIUS *with the second* SERVINGMAN.

60–1 ***tackle's torn ... noble vessel*** the metaphor is a naval one and shows that Aufidius recognises that although Coriolanus' clothes (rigging) are ragged, his body (ship) is that of a noble. The Elizabethans believed that appearance indicated one's nature,

AUFIDIUS
Where is this fellow?

2 SERVINGMAN
Here, sir; I'd have beaten him like a dog, but for disturbing the lords within.

AUFIDIUS
Whence com'st thou? What wouldst thou? Thy
name?
Why speak'st not? Speak, man. What's thy name?

CORIOLANUS
(*Unmuffling*) If, Tullus,
Not yet thou know'st me, and, seeing me, dost not
Think me for the man I am, necessity
Commands me name myself.

AUFIDIUS
What is thy name?

CORIOLANUS
A name unmusical to the Volscians' ears,
And harsh in sound to thine.

AUFIDIUS
Say, what's thy name?
Thou hast a grim appearance, and thy face
Bears a command in't; though thy tackle's torn,
Thou show'st a noble vessel. What's thy name?

CORIOLANUS
Prepare thy brow to frown – know'st thou me
yet?

AUFIDIUS
I know thee not. Thy name?

74 ***dastard*** cowardly. Coriolanus has become noticeably embittered against the patricians of the city.

84 ***heart of wreak*** heart favouring vengeance.

90 ***cank'red*** diseased.

spleen the part of the body seen as the source of ferocity.

91 ***under fiends*** devils.

CORIOLANUS

My name is Caius Marcius, who hath done
To thee particularly, and to all the Volsces,
Great hurt and mischief; thereto witness may
My surname, Coriolanus. The painful service,
The extreme dangers, and the drops of blood
Shed for my thankless country, are requited
But with that surname – a good memory
And witness of the malice and displeasure
Which thou shouldst bear me. Only that name
remains;
The cruelty and envy of the people,
Permitted by our dastard nobles, who
Have all forsook me, hath devour'd the rest,
And suffer'd me by th' voice of slaves to be
Whoop'd out of Rome. Now this extremity
Hath brought me to thy hearth; not out of
hope,
Mistake me not, to save my life; for if
I had fear'd death, of all the men i' th' world
I would have 'voided thee; but in mere spite,
To be full quit of those my banishers,
Stand I before thee here. Then if thou hast
A heart of wreak in thee, that wilt revenge
Thine own particular wrongs and stop those
maims
Of shame seen through thy country, speed thee
straight
And make my misery serve thy turn. So use it
That my revengeful services may prove
As benefits to thee; for I will fight
Against my cank'red country with the spleen
Of all the under fiends. But if so be

98 ***tuns*** barrels.

105–12 ***Let me . . . valour*** let me embrace that body which I have broken my lance against a hundred times; here I embrace the man who has been the target of my sword and swear a love as fervent as ever was my hate. Given Aufidius' pledge at the end of Act 1, the audience must question the sincerity of these words.

Thou dar'st not this, and that to prove more
fortunes
Th'art tir'd, then, in a word, I also am
Longer to live most weary, and present
My throat to thee and to thy ancient malice;
Which not to cut would show thee but a fool,
Since I have ever followed thee with hate,
Drawn tuns of blood out of thy country's breast,
And cannot live but to thy shame, unless
It be to do thee service.

AUFIDIUS

O Marcius, Marcius!
Each word thou hast spoke hath weeded from
my heart
A root of ancient envy. If Jupiter
Should from yond cloud speak divine things,
And say ''Tis true', I'd not believe them more
Than thee, all noble Marcius. Let me twine
Mine arms about that body, where against
My grained ash an hundred times hath broke
And scarr'd the moon with splinters; here I clip
The anvil of my sword, and do contest
As hotly and as nobly with thy love
As ever in ambitious strength I did
Contend against thy valour. Know thou first,
I lov'd the maid I married; never man
Sigh'd truer breath; but that I see thee here,
Thou noble thing, more dances my rapt heart
Than when I first my wedded mistress saw
Bestride my threshold. Why, thou Mars, I tell
thee
We have a power on foot, and I had purpose

130 ***o'erbea*** overcome it.

140–2 ***Whether to ... destroy*** Aufidius allows Coriolanus to guide him on whether to attack Rome outright or to conquer its outlying provinces, in order to give it a fright before destroying it. In accepting a subservient role, he appears to honour his guest, yet one must bear in mind the tribunes' description of Coriolanus' unassailability in serving under Cominius (Act I, scene I, lines 263–74) – a situation common to this one.

Once more to hew thy target from thy brawn,
Or lose mine arm for't. Thou hast beat me out
Twelve several times, and I have nightly since
Dreamt of encounters 'twixt thyself and me –
We have been down together in my sleep,
Unbuckling helms, fisting each other's throat –
And wak'd half dead with nothing. Worthy Marcius,
Had we no other quarrel else to Rome but that
Thou art thence banish'd, we would muster all
From twelve to seventy, and, pouring war
Into the bowels of ungrateful Rome,
Like a bold flood o'erbea. O, come, go in,
And take our friendly senators by th' hands,
Who now are here, taking their leaves of me
Who am prepar'd against your territories,
Though not for Rome itself.

CORIOLANUS

You bless me, gods!

AUFIDIUS

Therefore, most absolute sir, if thou wilt have
The leading of thine own revenges, take
Th' one half of my commission, and set down –
As best thou art experienc'd, since thou know'st
Thy country's strength and weakness – thine own ways,
Whether to knock against the gates of Rome,
Or rudely visit them in parts remote
To fright them ere destroy. But come in;
Let me commend thee first to those that shall
Say yea to thy desires. A thousand welcomes!
And more a friend than e'er an enemy;

161 ***wot*** a potential meaning is 'know'. The serving men are torn between their admiration for Coriolanus and their loyalty to their master: the strength of the former emotion is ominous, given the envious nature of Aufidius.

Yet, Marcius, that was much. Your hand; most
welcome!

Exeunt CORIOLANUS *and* AUFIDIUS

The two SERVINGMEN *come forward.*

1 SERVINGMAN

Here's a strange alteration!

2 SERVINGMAN

By my hand, I had thought to have strucken him with a cudgel; and yet my mind gave me his clothes made a false report of him.

1 SERVINGMAN

What an arm he has! He turn'd me about with his finger and his thumb, as one would set up a top.

2 SERVINGMAN

Nay, I knew by his face that there was something in him; he had, sir, a kind of face, methought – I cannot tell how to term it.

1 SERVINGMAN

He had so, looking as it were – Would I were hang'd, but I thought there was more in him than I could think.

2 SERVINGMAN

So did I, I'll be sworn. He is simply the rarest man i' th' world.

1 SERVINGMAN

I think he is; but a greater soldier than he you wot one.

173–4 ***I had as lief*** I would willingly rather be.

2 SERVINGMAN
Who, my master?

1 SERVINGMAN
Nay, it's no matter for that.

2 SERVINGMAN
Worth six on him.

1 SERVINGMAN
Nay, not so neither; but I take him to be the greater soldier.

2 SERVINGMAN
Faith, look you, one cannot tell how to say that; for the defence of a town our general is excellent.

1 SERVINGMAN
Ay, and for an assault too.

Re-enter the third SERVINGMAN.

3 SERVINGMAN
O slaves, I can tell you news – news, you rascals!

BOTH
What, what, what? Let's partake.

3 SERVINGMAN
I would not be a Roman, of all nations; I had as lief be a condemn'd man.

BOTH
Wherefore? wherefore?

3 SERVINGMAN
Why, here's he that was wont to thwack our general – Caius Marcius.

185–6 ***scotch'd . . . carbonado*** slashed and scarred him like a piece of cooked meat.

187 ***An he had . . . cannibally given*** if he had been given to cannibalism.

200 ***sowl*** shake.

1 SERVINGMAN
Why do you say 'thwack our general'?

3 SERVINGMAN
I do not say 'thwack our general', but he was always good enough for him.

2 SERVINGMAN
Come, we are fellows and friends. He was ever too hard for him, I have heard him say so himself.

1 SERVINGMAN
He was too hard for him directly, to say the troth on't; before Corioli he scotch'd him and notch'd him like a carbonado.

2 SERVINGMAN
An he had been cannibally given, he might have broil'd and eaten him too.

1 SERVINGMAN
But more of thy news!

3 SERVINGMAN
Why, he is so made on here within as if he were son and heir to Mars; set at upper end o' th' table; no question asked him by any of the senators but they stand bald before him. Our general himself makes a mistress of him, sanctifies himself with's hand, and turns up the white o' th' eye to his discourse. But the bottom of the news is, our general is cut i' th' middle and but one half of what he was yesterday, for the other has half by the entreaty and grant of the whole table. He'll go, he says, and sowl the porter of Rome gates by

207–8 ***directitude*** we share the first servant's bewilderment at what his companion means.

212 ***conies*** rabbits.

216 ***parcel*** portion.

th' ears; he will mow all down before him, and leave his passage poll'd.

2 SERVINGMAN

And he's as like to do't as any man I can imagine.

3 SERVINGMAN

Do't! He will do't; for look you, sir, he has as many friends as enemies; which friends, sir, as it were, durst not – look you, sir – show themselves, as we term it, his friends, whilest he's in directitude.

1 SERVINGMAN

Directitude? What's that?

3 SERVINGMAN

But when they shall see, sir, his crest up again and the man in blood, they will out of their burrows, like conies after rain, and revel all with him.

1 SERVINGMAN

But when goes this forward?

3 SERVINGMAN

To-morrow, to-day, presently. You shall have the drum struck up this afternoon; 'tis as it were a parcel of their feast, and to be executed ere they wipe their lips.

2 SERVINGMAN

Why, then we shall have a stirring world again. This peace is nothing but to rust iron, increase tailors, and breed balladmakers.

1 SERVINGMAN

Let me have war, say I; it exceeds peace as far as

224 ***mull'd*** dull'd (i.e. with wine).

2 ***His remedies are tame*** it is difficult to interpret this line exactly, although he appears to be saying that the dire consequences forecast at his expulsion, which the nobles hoped would lead to us repealing our order, have not happened.

day does night; it's spritely, waking, audible, and full of vent. Peace is a very apoplexy, lethargy; mull'd, deaf, sleepy, insensible; a getter of more bastard children than war's a destroyer of men.

2 SERVINGMAN
'Tis so; and as war in some sort may be said to be a ravisher, so it cannot be denied but peace is a great maker of cuckolds.

1 SERVINGMAN
Ay, and it makes men hate one another.

3 SERVINGMAN
Reason: because they then less need one another. The wars for my money. I hope to see Romans as cheap as Volscians. They are rising, they are rising.

BOTH
In, in, in, in!

Exeunt

Scene six

Rome. A public place.

Enter the two TRIBUNES, SICINIUS *and* BRUTUS.

SICINIUS
We hear not of him, neither need we fear him.
His remedies are tame. The present peace
And quietness of the people, which before
Were in wild hurry, here do make his friends
Blush that the world goes well; who rather had,

6–7 ***behold . . . streets*** see rebellious mobs obstructing the streets, i.e. so that they would have reason to rescind the edict of banishment.

18 ***nothing*** this is a further indication of how Coriolanus' resentment has grown. He had promised to keep in touch with his friends and relatives but now seems to have abandoned both.

Though they themselves did suffer by't, behold
Dissentious numbers pest'ring streets than see
Our tradesmen singing in their shops, and going
About their functions friendly.

Enter MENENIUS.

BRUTUS

We stood to't in good time. Is this Menenius?

SICINIUS

'Tis he, 'tis he. O, he is grown most kind
Of late. Hail, sir!

MENENIUS

Hail to you both!

SICINIUS

Your Coriolanus is not much miss'd
But with his friends. The commonwealth doth stand,
And so would do, were he more angry at it.

MENENIUS

All's well, and might have been much better if
He could have temporiz'd.

SICINIUS

Where is he, hear you?

MENENIUS

Nay, I hear nothing; his mother and his wife
Hear nothing from him.

Enter three or four CITIZENS.

CITIZENS

The gods preserve you both!

33–4 ***Self-loving . . . assistance*** the tribunes once more repeat their accusations, one of which is mistaken, the other trumped-up.

SICINIUS
God-den, our neighbours.

BRUTUS
God-den to you all, god-den to you all.

1 CITIZEN
Ourselves, our wives, and children, on our knees
Are bound to pray for you both.

SICINIUS
Live and thrive!

BRUTUS
Farewell, kind neighbours; we wish'd Coriolanus
Had lov'd you as we did.

CITIZENS
Now the gods keep you!

BOTH TRIBUNES
Farewell, farewell.

Exeunt CITIZENS

SICINIUS
This is a happier and more comely time
Than when these fellows ran about the streets
Crying confusion.

BRUTUS
Caius Marcius was
A worthy officer i' th' war, but insolent,
O'ercome with pride, ambitious past all thinking,
Self-loving –

SICINIUS
And affecting one sole throne,

44 ***Thrusts forth his horns*** Menenius compares him to a snail.

Without assistance.

MENENIUS

I think not so.

SICINIUS

We should by this, to all our lamentation,
If he had gone forth consul, found it so.

BRUTUS

The gods have well prevented it, and Rome
Sits safe and still without him.

Enter an ÆDILE.

ÆDILE

Worthy tribunes,
There is a slave, whom we have put in prison,
Reports the Volsces with two several powers
Are ent'red in the Roman territories,
And with the deepest malice of the war
Destroy what lies before 'em.

MENENIUS

'Tis Aufidius,
Who, hearing of our Marcius' banishment,
Thrusts forth his horns again into the world,
Which were inshell'd when Marcius stood for
Rome,
And durst not once peep out.

SICINIUS

Come, what talk you of Marcius?

BRUTUS

Go see this rumourer whipp'd. It cannot be
The Volsces dare break with us.

61 ***raising*** incitement.

MENENIUS

Cannot be!
We have record that very well it can;
And three examples of the like hath been
Within my age. But reason with the fellow
Before you punish him, where he heard this,
Lest you shall chance to whip your information
And beat the messenger who bids beware
Of what is to be dreaded.

SICINIUS

Tell not me.
I know this cannot be.

BRUTUS

Not possible.

Enter a MESSENGER.

MESSENGER

The nobles in great earnestness are going
All to the Senate House: some news is come
That turns their countenances.

SICINIUS

'Tis this slave –
Go whip him fore the people's eyes – his raising,
Nothing but his report.

MESSENGER

Yes, worthy sir,
The slave's report is seconded, and more,
More fearful, is deliver'd.

SICINIUS

What more fearful?

68–9 ***vows revenge . . . thing*** i.e. he intends to wipe out all of the populace.

74 ***Than violent'st contrariety*** opposite extremes.

MESSENGER

It is spoke freely out of many mouths –
How probable I do not know – that Marcius,
Join'd with Aufidius, leads a power 'gainst Rome,
And vows revenge as spacious as between
The young'st and oldest thing.

SICINIUS

This is most likely!

BRUTUS

Rais'd only that the weaker sort may wish
Good Marcius home again.

SICINIUS

The very trick on't.

MENENIUS

This is unlikely.
He and Aufidius can no more atone
Than violent'st contrariety.

Enter a second MESSENGER.

2 MESSENGER

You are sent for to the Senate.
A fearful army, led by Caius Marcius
Associated with Aufidius, rages
Upon our territories, and have already
O'erborne their way, consum'd with fire and took
What lay before them.

Enter COMINIUS.

COMINIUS

O, you have made good work!

87–8 ***Your franchises ... bore*** your liberties drastically reduced. (An auger is a carpenter's boring tool.)

97 ***apron men*** i.e. tradesmen.

MENENIUS

What news? what news?

COMINIUS

You have holp to ravish your own daughters and
To melt the city leads upon your pates,
To see your wives dishonour'd to your noses –

MENENIUS

What's the news? What's the news?

COMINIUS

Your temples burned in their cement, and
Your franchises, whereon you stood, confin'd
Into an auger's bore.

MENENIUS

Pray now, your news?
You have made fair work, I fear me. Pray, your news.
If Marcius should be join'd wi' th' Volscians –

COMINIUS

If!
He is their god; he leads them like a thing
Made by some other deity than Nature,
That shapes man better; and they follow him
Against us brats with no less confidence
Than boys pursuing summer butterflies,
Or butchers killing flies.

MENENIUS

You have made good work,
You and your apron men; you that stood so much

100 ***As Hercules . . . fruit*** refers to the last of Hercules' tasks, which was to gather golden apples from Hesperides, having first killed a dragon. The image echoes Coriolanus' description of both himself and the way Rome would fall.

104 ***smilingly revolt*** i.e. welcome him.

Upon the voice of occupation and
The breath of garlic-eaters!

COMINIUS

He'll shake
Your Rome about your ears.

MENENIUS

As Hercules
Did shake down mellow fruit. You have made fair work!

BRUTUS

But is this true, sir?

COMINIUS

Ay; and you'll look pale
Before you find it other. All the regions
Do smilingly revolt, and who resists
Are mock'd for valiant ignorance,
And perish constant fools. Who is't can blame him?
Your enemies and his find something in him.

MENENIUS

We are all undone unless
The noble man have mercy.

COMINIUS

Who shall ask it?
The tribunes cannot do't for shame; the people
Deserve such pity of him as the wolf
Does of the shepherds; for his best friends, if they
Should say 'Be good to Rome' – they charg'd him even

123 ***clusters*** crowds, swarms.

124 ***hoot*** a meaningless noise.

As those should do that had deserv'd his hate,
And therein show'd like enemies.

MENENIUS

'Tis true;
If he were putting to my house the brand
That should consume it, I have not the face
To say 'Beseech you, cease'. You have made fair hands,
You and your crafts! You have crafted fair!

COMINIUS

You have brought
A trembling upon Rome, such as was never
S' incapable of help.

BOTH TRIBUNES

Say not we brought it.

MENENIUS

How! Was't we? We lov'd him, but, like beasts
And cowardly nobles, gave way unto your clusters,
Who did hoot him out o' th' city.

COMINIUS

But I fear
They'll roar him in again. Tullus Aufidius,
The second name of men, obeys his points
As if he were his officer. Desperation
Is all the policy, strength, and defence,
That Rome can make against them.

Enter a troop of CITIZENS.

135 ***coxcombs*** heads.

MENENIUS

Here comes the clusters.
And is Aufidius with him? You are they
That made the air unwholesome when you cast
Your stinking greasy caps in hooting at
Coriolanus' exile. Now he's coming,
And not a hair upon a soldier's head
Which will not prove a whip; as many coxcombs
As you threw caps up will he tumble down,
And pay you for your voices. 'Tis no matter;
If he could burn us all into one coal,
We have deserv'd it.

PLEBEIANS

Faith, we hear fearful news.

1 CITIZEN

For mine own part,
When I said banish him, I said 'twas pity.

2 CITIZEN

And so did I.

3 CITIZEN

And so did I; and, to say the truth, so did very many of us. That we did, we did for the best; and though we willingly consented to his banishment, yet it was against our will.

COMINIUS

Y'are goodly things, you voices!

MENENIUS

You have made
Good work, you and your cry! Shall's to the Capitol?

155–6 ***I ever said ... him*** the citizens' reaction to the news once again shows their fickle natures.

160 ***Would half ... lie!*** if only half my wealth could be used to make this untrue! An interesting line because it shows that, despite his political status, Brutus is, in fact, of a different class from the peasants he represents. He is a symbol of the new middle class of Stuart England which used its mercantile wealth to exert political power.

COMINIUS

O, ay, what else?

Exeunt COMINIUS *and* MENENIUS

SICINIUS

Go masters, get you home; be not dismay'd;
These are a side that would be glad to have
This true which they so seem to fear. Go home,
And show no sign of fear.

1 CITIZEN

The gods be good to us! Come, masters, let's home. I ever said we were i' th' wrong when we banish'd him.

2 CITIZEN

So did we all. But come, let's home.

Exeunt CITIZENS

BRUTUS

I do not like this news.

SICINIUS

Nor I.

BRUTUS

Let's to the Capitol. Would half my wealth
Would buy this for a lie!

SICINIUS

Pray let's go.

Exeunt

1 ***th' Roman*** notice the disdain with which Aufidius speaks of Coriolanus when he is not present.

3 ***use him as the grace fore meat*** i.e. give him thanks before eating as if he were divine.

18 ***account*** day of reckoning.

Scene seven

A camp at a short distance from Rome.

Enter AUFIDIUS *with his* LIEUTENANT.

AUFIDIUS

Do they still fly to th' Roman?

LIEUTENANT

I do not know what witchcraft's in him, but
Your soldiers use him as the grace fore meat,
Their talk at table, and their thanks at end;
And you are dark'ned in this action, sir,
Even by your own.

AUFIDIUS

I cannot help it now,
Unless by using means I lame the foot
Of our design. He bears himself more proudlier,
Even to my person, than I thought he would
When first I did embrace him; yet his nature
In that's no changeling, and I must excuse
What cannot be amended.

LIEUTENANT

Yet I wish, sir –
I mean, for your particular – you had not
Join'd in commission with him, but either
Had borne the action of yourself, or else
To him had left it solely.

AUFIDIUS

I understand thee well; and be thou sure,
When he shall come to his account, he knows
not
What I can urge against him. Although it seems,

24–6 ***yet he hath ... account*** the threat is ominous, although it is unclear as to what Aufidius is referring.

35–48 ***First he was ... banish'd*** this is a valid judgement on his character. Aufidius' hesitation in saying whether Coriolanus has elements of all of these vices in him or merely one which has made him hated, reflects our own uncertainty about his character. It is an ambiguity the modern audience must resolve if he is to be seen as a tragic hero.

And so he thinks, and is no less apparent
To th' vulgar eye, that he bears all things fairly
And shows good husbandry for the Volscian
  state,
Fights dragon-like, and does achieve as soon
As draw his sword; yet he hath left undone
That which shall break his neck or hazard mine
Whene'er we come to our account.

LIEUTENANT

Sir, I beseech you, think you he'll carry Rome?

AUFIDIUS

All places yield to him ere he sits down,
And the nobility of Rome are his;
The senators and patricians love him too.
The tribunes are no soldiers, and their people
Will be as rash in the repeal as hasty
To expel him thence. I think he'll be to Rome
As is the osprey to the fish, who takes it
By sovereignty of nature. First he was
A noble servant to them, but he could not
Carry his honours even. Whether 'twas pride,
Which out of daily fortune ever taints
The happy man; whether defect of judgment,
To fail in the disposing of those chances
Which he was lord of; or whether nature,
Not to be other than one thing, not moving
From th' casque to th' cushion, but commanding
  peace
Even with the same austerity and garb
As he controll'd the war; but one of these –
As he hath spices of them all – not all,
For I dare so far free him – made him fear'd,

51–3 ***And power ... done*** power, which finds itself attractive, will find a way to be buried most quickly by praising itself.

So hated, and so banish'd. But he has a merit
To choke it in the utt'rance. So our virtues
Lie in th' interpretation of the time;
And power, unto itself most commendable,
Hath not a tomb so evident as a chair
T' extol what it hath done.
One fire drives out one fire; one nail, one nail;
Rights by rights falter, strengths by strengths do fail.
Come, let's away. When, Caius, Rome is thine,
Thou art poor'st of all; then shortly art thou mine.

Exeunt

Act 5: summary

Coriolanus is outside the gates of Rome at the head of a victorious Volscian army. Inside the city, all is confusion and panic. Cominius has been sent with a plea for mercy but has been rebuffed and now the tribunes are attempting to persuade Menenius to try. He accepts the mission and is confident of success; in contrast Cominius holds out little hope and goes to Volumnia to plead for her intercession.

Menenius meets with Coriolanus and is summarily dismissed. He is crushed by his failure and leaves to jeers. As Coriolanus pledges to accept no more emissaries, his mother, wife and son enter.

To dismiss the two men who meant most to him has been hard; to see his family kneeling before him all but destroys his resolve. Volumnia asks him to fulfil his filial duty of obedience to her. As a way out, she suggests he becomes an emissary of peace, praised by all. Although he realises that he will pay a heavy price for the action, he agrees.

In Rome, Menenius jeers at the panic-stricken Sicinius, more so when reports come of Brutus having been beaten by the mob. A messenger brings news of Volumnia's triumph and celebrations break out all over the city.

However, in Antium, Aufidius is plotting with conspirators and accuses Coriolanus of treachery. The city's judges accept the charge and set into action the judicial process but Aufidius will not wait for this and taunts Coriolanus in order to make him reveal his true self. The latter is infuriated and lashes out. He is hacked to pieces by the incensed crowd who surround him.

Aufidius, stands upon the corpse of his rival, but then appears to repent.

2 ***Which was sometime his general*** who was once his general, i.e. Cominius.

6 ***coy'd*** was reluctant.

13–15 ***He was . . . Rome*** out of respect to his new rulers, Marcius has dropped the surname of Coriolanus but will win a new title out of the ashes of Rome.

17 ***To make coals cheap*** i.e. for trivial gains. Although this is not a cause we have seen espoused, it is one which Menenius seizes on for its ironic value, given that Rome will soon burn.

Act Five

Scene one

Rome. A public place.

Enter MENENIUS, COMINIUS, SICINIUS *and* BRUTUS, *the two Tribunes, with others.*

MENENIUS

No, I'll not go. You hear what he hath said
Which was sometime his general, who lov'd him
In a most dear particular. He call'd me father;
But what o' that? Go, you that banish'd him:
A mile before his tent fall down, and knee
The way into his mercy. Nay, if he coy'd
To hear Cominius speak, I'll keep at home.

COMINIUS

He would not seem to know me.

MENENIUS

Do you hear?

COMINIUS

Yet one time he did call me by my name.
I urg'd our old acquaintance, and the drops
That we have bled together. 'Coriolanus'
He would not answer to; forbad all names;
He was a kind of nothing, titleless,
Till he had forg'd himself a name i' th' fire
Of burning Rome.

MENENIUS

Why, so! You have made good work.
A pair of tribunes that have wrack'd for Rome
To make coals cheap – a noble memory!

20 ***bare petition*** i) shameful; ii) threadbare, i.e. pointless.

25–8 ***He could . . . th' offence*** Coriolanus uses a metaphor which shows his continuing contempt for the nobles who have mixed with the 'musty chaff' of the populace. However, it also shows a callous disregard for the value of human life, particularly as his wife, mother and child are included in his potential victims.

34 ***In this so never-needed help*** in this time when help was never so much needed.

38 ***our countryman*** the hypocrisy is all too evident in this title.

COMINIUS

I minded him how royal 'twas to pardon
When it was less expected; he replied,
It was a bare petition of a state
To one whom they had punish'd.

MENENIUS

Very well.
Could he say less?

COMINIUS

I offer'd to awaken his regard
For's private friends; his answer to me was,
He could not stay to pick them in a pile
Of noisome musty chaff. He said 'twas folly,
For one poor grain or two, to leave unburnt
And still to nose th' offence.

MENENIUS

For one poor grain or two!
I am one of those. His mother, wife, his child,
And this brave fellow too – we are the grains:
You are the musty chaff, and you are smelt
Above the moon. We must be burnt for you.

SICINIUS

Nay, pray be patient; if you refuse your aid
In this so never-needed help, yet do not
Upbraid's with our distress. But sure, if you
Would be your country's pleader, your good tongue,
More than the instant army we can make,
Might stop our countryman.

46 ***after the measure*** in proportion to the good will.

MENENIUS

No; I'll not meddle.

SICINIUS

Pray you go to him.

MENENIUS

What should I do?

BRUTUS

Only make trial what your love can do
For Rome, towards Marcius.

MENENIUS

Well, and say that Marcius
Return me, as Cominius is return'd,
Unheard – what then?
But as a discontented friend, grief-shot
With his unkindness? Say't be so?

SICINIUS

Yet your good will
Must have that thanks from Rome after the measure
As you intended well.

MENENIUS

I'll undertake't;
I think he'll hear me. Yet to bite his lip
And hum at good Cominius much unhearts me.
He was not taken well; he had not din'd;
The veins unfill'd, our blood is cold, and then
We pout upon the morning, are unapt
To give or to forgive; but when we have stuff'd
These pipes and these conveyances of our blood
With wine and feeding, we have suppler souls

67–9 ***What he . . . conditions*** although the phrasing is tortuous, the sense is that Coriolanus has put in writing his conditions for leaving Rome standing, stating exactly what he will and will not do.

Than in our priest-like fasts. Therefore I'll watch
him
Till he be dieted to my request,
And then I'll set upon him.

BRUTUS

You know the very road into his kindness
And cannot lose your way.

MENENIUS

Good faith, I'll prove him,
Speed how it will. I shall ere long have knowledge
Of my success.

Exit

COMINIUS

He'll never hear him.

SICINIUS

Not?

COMINIUS

I tell you he does sit in gold, his eye
Red as 'twould burn Rome, and his injury
The gaoler to his pity. I kneel'd before him;
'Twas very faintly he said 'Rise'; dismiss'd me
Thus with his speechless hand. What he would do,
He sent in writing after me; what he would not,
Bound with an oath to yield to his conditions;
So that all hope is vain,
Unless his noble mother and his wife,
Who, as I hear, mean to solicit him
For mercy to his country. Therefore let's hence,
And with our fair entreaties haste them on.

Exeunt

10 ***lots to blanks*** the chances are/the odds are.

Scene two

The Volscian camp before Rome.

Enter MENENIUS *to the Watch on guard.*

1 WATCHMAN
Stay. Whence are you?

2 WATCHMAN
Stand, and go back.

MENENIUS
You guard like men, 'tis well; but, by your leave,
I am an officer of state and come
To speak with Coriolanus.

1 WATCHMAN
From whence?

MENENIUS
From Rome.

1 WATCHMAN
You may not pass; you must return. Our general
Will no more hear from thence.

2 WATCHMAN
You'll see your Rome embrac'd with fire before
You'll speak with Coriolanus.

MENENIUS
Good my friends,
If you have heard your general talk of Rome
And of his friends there, it is lots to blanks
My name hath touch'd your ears: it is Menenius.

13 ***passable*** acceptable as a password.

14–16 ***I have ... amplified*** Menenius places much store by the esteem in which he always held Coriolanus.

18–19 ***with all ... suffer*** to the full extent I can without resorting to lying.

20–2 ***Like to a bowl ... leasing*** I have gone too far in praising him, almost to the point of telling lies.

1 WATCHMAN
Be it so; go back. The virtue of your name
Is not here passable.

MENENIUS
I tell thee, fellow,
Thy general is my lover. I have been
The book of his good acts whence men have read
His fame unparallel'd haply amplified;
For I have ever verified my friends –
Of whom he's chief – with all the size that verity
Would without lapsing suffer. Nay, sometimes,
Like to a bowl upon a subtle ground,
I have tumbled past the throw, and in his praise
Have almost stamp'd the leasing; therefore, fellow,
I must have leave to pass.

1 WATCHMAN
Faith, sir, if you had told as many lies in his behalf as you have uttered words in your own, you should not pass here; no, though it were as virtuous to lie as to live chastely. Therefore go back.

MENENIUS
Prithee, fellow, remember my name is Menenius, always factionary on the party of your general.

2 WATCHMAN
Howsoever you have been his liar, as you say you have, I am one that, telling true under him, must say you cannot pass. Therefore go back.

41 ***your shield*** i.e. Coriolanus, the most effective defence Rome had.

43 ***virginal palms*** i.e. held up in pleading for mercy.

44–5 ***decay'd dotant*** ageing fool – the alliteration is a clear indication of the man's scorn.

53 ***estimation*** respect.

MENENIUS

Has he din'd, canst thou tell? For I would not speak with him till after dinner.

1 WATCHMAN

You are a Roman, are you?

MENENIUS

I am as thy general is.

1 WATCHMAN

Then you should hate Rome, as he does. Can you, when you have push'd out your gates the very defender of them, and in a violent popular ignorance given your enemy your shield, think to front his revenges with the easy groans of old women, the virginal palms of your daughters, or with the palsied intercession of such a decay'd dotant as you seem to be? Can you think to blow out the intended fire your city is ready to flame in with such weak breath as this? No, you are deceiv'd; therefore back to Rome and prepare for your execution. You are condemn'd; our general has sworn you out of reprieve and pardon.

MENENIUS

Sirrah, if thy captain knew I were here, he would use me with estimation.

1 WATCHMAN

Come, my captain knows you not.

MENENIUS

I mean thy general.

63 ***a Jack guardant*** jumped-up guard.

1 WATCHMAN

My general cares not for you. Back, I say; go, lest I let forth your half pint of blood. Back – that's the utmost of your having. Back.

MENENIUS

Nay, but fellow, fellow –

Enter CORIOLANUS *with* AUFIDIUS.

CORIOLANUS

What's the matter?

MENENIUS

Now, you companion, I'll say an errand for you; you shall know now that I am in estimation; you shall perceive that a Jack guardant cannot office me from my son Coriolanus. Guess but by my entertainment with him if thou stand'st not i' th' state of hanging, or of some death more long in spectatorship and crueller in suffering; behold now presently, and swoon for what's to come upon thee. The glorious gods sit in hourly synod about thy particular prosperity, and love thee no worse than thy old father Menenius does! O my son! my son! thou art preparing fire for us; look thee, here's water to quench it. I was hardly moved to come to thee; but being assured none but myself could move thee, I have been blown out of your gates with sighs, and conjure thee to pardon Rome and thy petitionary countrymen. The good gods assuage thy wrath, and turn the dregs of it upon this varlet here; this, who, like a block, hath denied my access to thee.

86–8 ***That we have . . . much*** the memory that we have been friends will be lost in the thought of your ungrateful forgetfulness, rather than be aroused by any pity in me now.

CORIOLANUS
Away!

MENENIUS
How! away!

CORIOLANUS
Wife, mother, child, I know not. My affairs
Are servanted to others. Though I owe
My revenge properly, my remission lies
In Volscian breasts. That we have been familiar,
Ingrate forgetfulness shall poison rather
Than pity note how much. Therefore be gone.
Mine ears against your suits are stronger than
Your gates against my force. Yet, for I lov'd thee,
Take this along; I writ it for thy sake (*Gives a letter*).
And would have sent it. Another word,
Menenius,
I will not hear thee speak. This man, Aufidius,
Was my belov'd in Rome; yet thou behold'st.

AUFIDIUS
You keep a constant temper.

Exeunt CORIOLANUS *and* AUFIDIUS

1 WATCHMAN
Now, sir, is your name Menenius?

2 WATCHMAN
'Tis a spell, you see, of much power! You know the way home again.

1 WATCHMAN
Do you hear how we are shent for keeping your greatness back?

110–11 ***The worthy ... wind-shaken*** the scene ends on an ominous note for Coriolanus, particularly as we know that Aufidius is lying in wait for him.

2 WATCHMAN

What cause, do you think, I have to swoon?

MENENIUS

I neither care for th' world nor your general; for such things as you, I can scarce think there's any, y'are so slight. He that hath a will to die by himself fears it not from another. Let your general do his worst. For you, be that you are, long; and your misery increase with your age! I say to you, as I was said to: Away!

Exit

1 WATCHMAN

A noble fellow, I warrant him.

2 WATCHMAN

The worthy fellow is our general; he's the rock, the oak not to be wind-shaken.

Exeunt

Scene three

The tent of Coriolanus.

Enter CORIOLANUS, AUFIDIUS, *and others.*

CORIOLANUS

We will before the walls of Rome to-morrow
Set down our host. My partner in this action,
You must report to th' Volscian lords how plainly
I have borne this business.

AUFIDIUS

Only their ends
You have respected; stopp'd your ears against

11 ***godded*** made a god out of.

25 ***bond and privilege of nature*** bonds of childhood; natural ties.

The general suit of Rome; never admitted
A private whisper – no, not with such friends
That thought them sure of you.

CORIOLANUS

This last old man,
Whom with a crack'd heart I have sent to Rome,
Lov'd me above the measure of a father;
Nay, godded me indeed. Their latest refuge
Was to send him; for whose old love I have –
Though I show'd sourly to him – once more offer'd
The first conditions, which they did refuse
And cannot now accept. To grace him only,
That thought he could do more, a very little
I have yielded to; fresh embassies and suits,
Nor from the state nor private friends, hereafter
Will I lend ear to. (*Shout within*) Ha! what shout is this?
Shall I be tempted to infringe my vow
In the same time 'tis made? I will not.

Enter, in mourning habits, VIRGILIA, VOLUMNIA, VALERIA, YOUNG MARCIUS, *with Attendants.*

My wife comes foremost, then the honour'd mould
Wherein this trunk was fram'd, and in her hand
The grandchild to her blood. But out, affection!
All bond and privilege of nature, break!
Let it be virtuous to be obstinate.
What is that curtsy worth? or those doves' eyes,
Which can make gods forsworn? I melt, and am not

30 ***Olympus*** the mountain which was home to the gods.

35 ***stand*** stand firm.

41 ***I am out*** speechless.

51–2 ***Of thy . . . sons*** Coriolanus is addressing his knee, saying that it should make a deeper mark when giving homage to his mother than that of other sons.

Of stronger earth than others. My mother bows,
As if Olympus to a molehill should
In supplication nod; and my young boy
Hath an aspect of intercession which
Great nature cries 'Deny not'. Let the Volsces
Plough Rome and harrow Italy; I'll never
Be such a gosling to obey instinct, but stand
As if a man were author of himself
And knew no other kin.

VIRGILIA

My lord and husband!

CORIOLANUS

These eyes are not the same I wore in Rome.

VIRGILIA

The sorrow that delivers us thus chang'd
Makes you think so.

CORIOLANUS

Like a dull actor now
I have forgot my part and I am out,
Even to a full disgrace. Best of my flesh,
Forgive my tyranny; but do not say,
For that, 'Forgive our Romans'. O, a kiss
Long as my exile, sweet as my revenge!
Now, by the jealous queen of heaven, that kiss
I carried from thee, dear, and my true lip
Hath virgin'd it e'er since. You gods! I prate,
And the most noble mother of the world
Leave unsaluted. Sink, my knee, i' th' earth;
(*Kneels*)
Of thy deep duty more impression show
Than that of common sons.

55 ***as mistaken all this while*** as having been mistaken all this time. She turns his homage upon him in order to weaken his resolve.

58–60 ***Then let . . . fiery sun*** Coriolanus, shocked by the action, says that now even the impossible can happen. He likens the image of a mother kneeling before her son to pebbles replacing stars and the winds destroying the sun by throwing trees against it.

65 ***The moon of Rome . . . temple*** Coriolanus commends Valeria as a pure maiden in strangely lyrical terms, comparing her to the icicles which hang upon the temple of Diana, goddess of chastity. He is evidently moved by the sight of Roman femininity, in the form of a mother, wife and virgin, begging before him.

68 ***a poor epitome of yours*** an abridged version of yourself, i.e. his son.

VOLUMNIA

O, stand up blest!
Whilst with no softer cushion than the flint
I kneel before thee, and unproperly
Show duty, as mistaken all this while
Between the child and parent. (*Kneels*)

CORIOLANUS

What's this?
Your knees to me, to your corrected son?
Then let the pebbles on the hungry beach
Fillip the stars; then let the mutinous winds
Strike the proud cedars 'gainst the fiery sun,
Murd'ring impossibility, to make
What cannot be slight work.

VOLUMNIA

Thou art my warrior;
I holp to frame thee. Do you know this lady?

CORIOLANUS

The noble sister of Publicola,
The moon of Rome, chaste as the icicle
That's curdied by the frost from purest snow,
And hangs on Dian's temple – dear Valeria!

VOLUMNIA

This is a poor epitome of yours,
Which by th' interpretation of full time
May show like all yourself.

CORIOLANUS

The god of soldiers,
With the consent of supreme Jove, inform
Thy thoughts with nobleness, that thou mayst prove

74 ***sea-mark*** landmark used by sailors to give them their bearings.

To shame unvulnerable, and stick i' th' wars
Like a great sea-mark, standing every flaw,
And saving those that eye thee!

VOLUMNIA

Your knee, sirrah.

CORIOLANUS

That's my brave boy.

VOLUMNIA

Even he, your wife, this lady, and myself,
Are suitors to you.

CORIOLANUS

I beseech you, peace!
Or, if you'd ask, remember this before:
The thing I have forsworn to grant may never
Be held by you denials. Do not bid me
Dismiss my soldiers, or capitulate
Again with Rome's mechanics. Tell me not
Wherein I seem unnatural; desire not
T'allay my rages and revenges with
Your colder reasons.

VOLUMNIA

O, no more, no more!
You have said you will not grant us any thing –
For we have nothing else to ask but that
Which you deny already; yet we will ask,
That, if you fail in our request, the blame
May hang upon your hardness; therefore hear
us.

CORIOLANUS

Aufidius, and you Volsces, mark; for we'll

94 ***raiment*** neglected clothes.

104 ***capital*** fatal.

112 ***An evident calamity*** a manifest tragedy. Volumnia points out that the family of Coriolanus are in a no win situation: if he is successful, they will die; if he fails, they will see him chained and then executed.

Hear nought from Rome in private. Your
request?

VOLUMNIA

Should we be silent and not speak, our raiment
And state of bodies would bewray what life
We have led since thy exile. Think with thyself
How more unfortunate than all living women
Are we come hither; since that thy sight, which
should
Make our eyes flow with joy, hearts dance with
comforts,
Constrains them weep and shake with fear and
sorrow,
Making the mother, wife, and child, to see
The son, the husband, and the father, tearing
His country's bowels out. And to poor we
Thine enmity's most capital: thou bar'st us
Our prayers to the gods, which is a comfort
That all but we enjoy. For how can we,
Alas, how can we for our country pray,
Whereto we are bound, together with thy victory,
Whereto we are bound? Alack, or we must lose
The country, our dear nurse, or else thy person,
Our comfort in the country. We must find
An evident calamity, though we had
Our wish, which side should win; for either thou
Must as a foreign recreant be led
With manacles through our streets, or else
Triumphantly tread on thy country's ruin,
And bear the palm for having bravely shed
Thy wife and children's blood. For myself, son,
I purpose not to wait on fortune till

124 ***on thy mother's womb*** although the meaning of her speech is not clear in a literal sense, the image she uses is horrific.

These wars determine; if I can not persuade thee
Rather to show a noble grace to both parts
Than seek the end of one, thou shalt no sooner
March to assault thy country than to tread –
Trust to't, thou shalt not – on thy mother's womb
That brought thee to this world.

VIRGILIA

Ay, and mine,
That brought you forth this boy to keep your name
Living to time.

BOY

'A shall not tread on me!
I'll run away till I am bigger, but then I'll fight.

CORIOLANUS

Not of a woman's tenderness to be
Requires nor child nor woman's face to see.
I have sat too long. (*Rising*)

VOLUMNIA

Nay, go not from us thus.
If it were so that our request did tend
To save the Romans, thereby to destroy
The Volsces whom you serve, you might condemn us
As poisonous of your honour. No, our suit
Is that you reconcile them: while the Volsces
May say 'This mercy we have show'd', the Romans
'This we receiv'd', and each in either side
Give the all-hail to thee, and cry 'Be blest

150–3 ***To imitate . . . oak*** Volumnia attempts to show Coriolanus that to make peace would be honourable by comparing the action to Jove, the father of the gods, who was reputed to be able to throw thunderbolts to earth. His action would be similar in that it would indicate the wielding of huge strength whilst actually causing little damage.

160 ***Like one i' th' stocks*** anachronistic image pertaining to vagrants, left in the stocks and ignored.

For making up this peace!' Thou know'st, great son,
The end of war's uncertain; but this certain,
That, if thou conquer Rome, the benefit
Which thou shalt thereby reap is such a name
Whose repetition will be dogg'd with curses;
Whose chronicle thus writ: 'The man was noble,
But with his last attempt he wip'd it out,
Destroy'd his country, and his name remains
To th' ensuing age abhorr'd'. Speak to me, son.
Thou hast affected the fine strains of honour,
To imitate the graces of the gods,
To tear with thunder the wide cheeks o' th' air,
And yet to charge thy sulphur with a bolt
That should but rive an oak. Why dost not speak?
Think'st thou it honourable for a noble man
Still to remember wrongs? Daughter, speak you:
He cares not for your weeping. Speak thou, boy;
Perhaps thy childishness will move him more
Than can our reasons. There's no man in the world
More bound to's mother, yet here he lets me prate
Like one i' th' stocks. Thou hast never in thy life
Show'd thy dear mother any courtesy,
When she, poor hen, fond of no second brood,
Has cluck'd thee to the wars, and safely home
Loaden with honour. Say my request's unjust,
And spurn me back; but if it be not so,
Thou art not honest, and the gods will plague thee,
That thou restrain'st from me the duty which
To a mother's part belongs. He turns away.

176 ***reason our petition*** i.e. by his action and relationship to you gives more force to our petition.

194 ***withal*** with it.

Down, ladies; let us shame him with our knees.
To his surname Coriolanus 'longs more pride
Than pity to our prayers. Down. An end;
This is the last. So we will home to Rome,
And die among our neighbours. Nay, behold's!
This boy, that cannot tell what he would have
But kneels and holds up hands for fellowship,
Does reason our petition with more strength
Than thou hast to deny't. Come, let us go.
This fellow had a Volscian to his mother;
His wife is in Corioli, and his child
Like him by chance. Yet give us our dispatch.
I am hush'd until our city be afire,
And then I'll speak a little.

He holds her by the hand, silent.

CORIOLANUS

O mother, mother!
What have you done? Behold, the heavens do ope,
The gods look down, and this unnatural scene
They laugh at. O my mother, mother! O!
You have won a happy victory to Rome;
But for your son – believe it, O, believe it! –
Most dangerously you have with him prevail'd,
If not most mortal to him. But let it come.
Aufidius, though I cannot make true wars,
I'll frame convenient peace. Now, good Aufidius,
Were you in my stead, would you have heard
A mother less, or granted less, Aufidius?

AUFIDIUS

I was mov'd withal.

199 ***Stand to me in this cause*** support me in this matter.

206 ***counter-seal'd*** i.e., sealed so that Rome knows it is genuine.

CORIOLANUS

I dare be sworn you were!
And, sir, it is no little thing to make
Mine eyes to sweat compassion. But, good sir,
What peace you'll make, advise me. For my part,
I'll not to Rome, I'll back with you; and pray you
Stand to me in this cause. O mother! wife!

AUFIDIUS

(*Aside*) I am glad thou hast set thy mercy and thy
honour
At difference in thee. Out of that I'll work
Myself a former fortune.

CORIOLANUS

(*To the ladies*) Ay, by and by;
But we will drink together; and you shall bear
A better witness back than words, which we,
On like conditions, will have counter-seal'd.
Come, enter with us. Ladies, you deserve
To have a temple built you. All the swords
In Italy, and her confederate arms,
Could not have made this peace.

Exeunt

1 ***coign*** cornerstone.

Scene four

Rome. A public place.

Enter MENENIUS *and* SICINIUS.

MENENIUS

See you yond coign o' th' Capitol, yond corner-stone?

SICINIUS

Why, what of that?

MENENIUS

If it be possible for you to displace it with your little finger, there is some hope the ladies of Rome, especially his mother, may prevail with him. But I say there is no hope in't; our throats are sentenc'd, and stay upon execution.

SICINIUS

Is't possible that so short a time can alter the condition of a man?

MENENIUS

There is differency between a grub and a butterfly; yet your butterfly was a grub. This Marcius is grown from man to dragon; he has wings, he's more than a creeping thing.

SICINIUS

He lov'd his mother dearly.

MENENIUS

So did he me; and he no more remembers his mother now than an eight-year-old horse. The tartness of his face sours ripe grapes; when he walks, he moves like an engine and the ground

20–1 ***pierce a corslet*** pierce body-armour.

21 ***knell*** i.e. a bell knelling someone's death.

23 ***Alexander*** like a statue of Alexander the Great.

shrinks before his treading. He is able to pierce a corslet with his eye, talks like a knell, and his hum is a battery. He sits in his state as a thing made for Alexander. What he bids be done is finish'd with his bidding. He wants nothing of a god but eternity, and a heaven to throne in.

SICINIUS

Yes – mercy, if you report him truly.

MENENIUS

I paint him in the character. Mark what mercy his mother shall bring from him. There is no more mercy in him than there is milk in a male tiger; that shall our poor city find. And all this is 'long of you.

SICINIUS

The gods be good unto us!

MENENIUS

No, in such a case the gods will not be good unto us. When we banish'd him we respected not them; and, he returning to break our necks, they respect not us.

Enter a MESSENGER.

MESSENGER

Sir, if you'd save your life, fly to your house.
The plebeians have got your fellow tribune
And hale him up and down; all swearing if
The Roman ladies bring not comfort home
They'll give him death by inches.

Enter another MESSENGER.

43 ***dislodg'd*** i.e. gone from their camp.

51 ***sackbuts, psalteries, and fifes*** loud brass trumpets, stringed instruments and drums.

SICINIUS

What's the news?

2 MESSENGER

Good news, good news! The ladies have prevail'd,
The Volscians are dislodg'd, and Marcius gone.
A merrier day did never yet greet Rome,
No, not th' expulsion of the Tarquins.

SICINIUS

Friend,
Art thou certain this is true? Is't most certain?

2 MESSENGER

As certain as I know the sun is fire.
Where have you lurk'd, that you make doubt of it?
Ne'er through an arch so hurried the blown tide
As the recomforted through th' gates. Why, hark you!

Trumpets, hautboys, drums beat, all together.

The trumpets, sackbuts, psalteries, and fifes,
Tabors and cymbals, and the shouting Romans,
Make the sun dance. Hark you!

A shout within.

MENENIUS

This is good news.
I will go meet the ladies. This Volumnia
Is worth of consuls, senators, patricians,
A city full; of tribunes such as you,
A sea and land full. You have pray'd well to-day:

59 ***doit*** a small coin of virtually no value.

This morning for ten thousand of your throats
I'd not have given a doit. Hark, how they joy!

Music still with the shouts.

SICINIUS
First, the gods bless you for your tidings; next,
Accept my thankfulness.

2 MESSENGER
Sir, we have all
Great cause to give great thanks.

SICINIUS
They are near the city?

MESSENGER
Almost at point to enter.

SICINIUS
We'll meet them,
And help the joy.

Exeunt

Scene five

Rome. A street near the gate.

Enter two SENATORS *with* VOLUMNIA, VIRGILIA, VALERIA, *passing over the stage, with other Lords.*

1 SENATOR
Behold our patroness, the life of Rome!
Call all your tribes together, praise the gods,
And make triumphant fires; strew flowers before
them.

5 ***Him*** the one I accuse.

6 ***ports*** gates.

9–11 ***Even so . . . slain*** like one who has been poisoned by his own benevolence and slain by his own charitable act.

Unshout the noise that banish'd Marcius,
Repeal him with the welcome of his mother;
Cry 'Welcome, ladies, welcome!'

ALL

Welcome, ladies,
Welcome!

A flourish with drums and trumpets. Exeunt

Scene six

Corioli. A public place.

Enter TULLUS AUFIDIUS, *with Attendants.*

AUFIDIUS

Go tell the lords o' th' city I am here;
Deliver them this paper; having read it,
Bid them repair to th' market-place, where I,
Even in theirs and in the commons' ears,
Will vouch the truth of it. Him I accuse
The city ports by this hath enter'd and
Intends t' appear before the people, hoping
To purge himself with words. Dispatch.

Exeunt Attendants

Enter three or four CONSPIRATORS *of Aufidius' faction.*

Most welcome!

1 CONSPIRATOR

How is it with our general?

AUFIDIUS

Even so

19–20 ***And my pretext … construction*** my plan for striking at him can be interpreted as an honourable act.

As with a man by his own alms empoison'd,
And with his charity slain.

2 CONSPIRATOR

Most noble sir,
If you do hold the same intent wherein
You wish'd us parties, we'll deliver you
Of your great danger.

AUFIDIUS

Sir, I cannot tell;
We must proceed as we do find the people.

3 CONSPIRATOR

The people will remain uncertain whilst
'Twixt you there's difference; but the fall of
either
Makes the survivor heir of all.

AUFIDIUS

I know it;
And my pretext to strike at him admits
A good construction. I rais'd him, and I pawn'd
Mine honour for his truth; who being so
heighten'd,
He watered his new plants with dews of flattery,
Seducing so my friends; and to this end
He bow'd his nature, never known before
But to be rough, unswayable, and free.

3 CONSPIRATOR

Sir, his stoutness
When he did stand for consul, which he lost
By lack of stooping –

40 ***mercenary*** hired soldier.

44 ***my sinews will be stretch'd upon*** my strength will be strained against.

45 ***women's rheum*** women's tears.

AUFIDIUS

That I would have spoke of.
Being banish'd for't, he came unto my hearth,
Presented to my knife his throat. I took him;
Made him joint-servant with me; gave him way
In all his own desires; nay, let him choose
Out of my files, his projects to accomplish,
My best and freshest men; serv'd his designments
In mine own person; holp to reap the fame
Which he did end all his, and took some pride
To do myself this wrong. Till, at the last,
I seem'd his follower, not partner; and
He wag'd me with his countenance as if
I had been mercenary.

1 CONSPIRATOR

So he did, my lord.
The army marvell'd at it; and, in the last,
When he had carried Rome and that we look'd
For no less spoil than glory –

AUFIDIUS

There was it;
For which my sinews shall be stretch'd upon him.
At a few drops of women's rheum, which are
As cheap as lies, he sold the blood and labour
Of our great action; therefore shall he die,
And I'll renew me in his fall. But, hark!

Drums and trumpets sound, with great shouts of the people.

1 CONSPIRATOR
Your native town you enter'd like a post,
And had no welcomes home; but he returns
Splitting the air with noise.

56–8 ***When he lies . . . body*** when he lies dead, you can tell his story how you like and so bury along with his body his reasons for acting the way he did.

64 ***easy fines*** gentle punishment.

65–8 ***give away . . . charge*** give away the advantages reaped from our raising of an army, acting with the authority which we had given him.

2 CONSPIRATOR

And patient fools,
Whose children he hath slain, their base throats tear
With giving him glory.

3 CONSPIRATOR

Therefore, at your vantage,
Ere he express himself or move the people
With what he would say, let him feel your sword,
Which we will second. When he lies along,
After your way his tale pronounc'd shall bury
His reasons with his body.

AUFIDIUS

Say no more:
Here come the lords.

Enter the Lords of the city.

LORDS

You are most welcome home.

AUFIDIUS

I have not deserv'd it.
But, worthy lords, have you with heed perused
What I have written to you?

LORDS

We have.

1 LORD

And grieve to hear't.
What faults he made before the last, I think
Might have found easy fines; but there to end
Where he was to begin, and give away

67–8 ***making a treaty . . . yielding*** making a treaty when there was an opportunity for conquest.

76–8 ***Our spoils . . . action*** the spoils of our conquests more than meet a third part of the expenses of our campaign.

The benefit of our levies, answering us
With our own charge, making a treaty where
There was a yielding – this admits no excuse.

AUFIDIUS

He approaches; you shall hear him.

Enter CORIOLANUS, *marching with drum and colours: the Commoners being with him.*

CORIOLANUS

Hail, lords! I am return'd your soldier;
No more infected with my country's love
Than when I parted hence, but still subsisting
Under your great command. You are to know
That prosperously I have attempted, and
With bloody passage led your wars even to
The gates of Rome. Our spoils we have brought home
Doth more than counterpoise a full third part
The charges of the action. We have made peace
With no less honour to the Antiates
Than shame to th' Romans; and we here deliver,
Subscrib'd by th' consuls and patricians,
Together with the seal o' th' Senate, what
We have compounded on.

AUFIDIUS

Read it not, noble lords;
But tell the traitor in the highest degree
He hath abus'd your powers.

CORIOLANUS

Traitor! How now?

86 ***Marcius!*** Coriolanus regards the omission of his surname as disrespectful. We can sense his anger rising, which is exactly what Aufidius wants.

90 ***perfidiously*** treacherously.

92 ***drops of salt*** tears.

95–6 ***never admitting . . . war*** never consulting with his fellow generals.

96–99 ***but at his . . . others*** is the exaggeration intended to convince the city judges or to anger Coriolanus?

AUFIDIUS

Ay, traitor, Marcius.

CORIOLANUS

Marcius!

AUFIDIUS

Ay, Marcius, Caius Marcius! Dost thou think
I'll grace thee with that robbery, thy stol'n name
Coriolanus, in Corioli?
You lords and heads o' th' state, perfidiously
He has betray'd your business and given up,
For certain drops of salt, your city Rome –
I say your city – to his wife and mother;
Breaking his oath and resolution like
A twist of rotten silk; never admitting
Counsel o' th' war; but at his nurse's tears
He whin'd and roar'd away your victory,
That pages blush'd at him, and men of heart
Look'd wond'ring each at others.

CORIOLANUS

Hear'st thou, Mars?

AUFIDIUS

Name not the god, thou boy of tears –

CORIOLANUS

Ha!

AUFIDIUS

– no more.

CORIOLANUS

Measureless liar, thou hast made my heart
Too great for what contains it. 'Boy'! O slave!

104 ***scold*** either Coriolanus has learned nothing from his experiences or he is being deliberately untruthful.

123–4 ***his fame folds . . . th' earth*** he is famous throughout all of the earth

Pardon me, lords, 'tis the first time that ever
I was forc'd to scold. Your judgments, my grave lords,
Must give this cur the lie; and his own notion –
Who wears my stripes impress'd upon him, that
Must bear my beating to his grave – shall join
To thrust the lie unto him.

1 LORD
Peace, both, and hear me speak.

CORIOLANUS
Cut me to pieces, Volsces; men and lads,
Stain all your edges on me. 'Boy'! False hound!
If you have writ your annals true, 'tis there
That, like an eagle in a dove-cote, I
Flutter'd your Volscians in Corioli.
Alone I did it. 'Boy'!

AUFIDIUS
Why, noble lords,
Will you be put in mind of his blind fortune,
Which was your shame, by this unholy braggart,
Fore your own eyes and ears?

CONSPIRATORS
Let him die for't.

ALL THE PEOPLE
Tear him to pieces. Do it presently. He kill'd my son. My daughter. He kill'd my cousin Marcus. He kill'd my father.

2 LORD
Peace, ho! No outrage – peace!
The man is noble, and his fame folds in

133 ***Tread not upon him*** this suggests that Aufidius has trodden upon the corpse in triumph.

This orb o' th' earth. His last offences to us
Shall have judicious hearing. Stand, Aufidius,
And trouble not the peace.

CORIOLANUS

O that I had him,
With six Aufidiuses, or more – his tribe,
To use my lawful sword!

AUFIDIUS

Insolent villain!

CONSPIRATORS

Kill, kill, kill, kill, kill him!

The CONSPIRATORS *draw and kill* CORIOLANUS, *who falls.* AUFIDIUS *stands on him.*

LORDS

Hold, hold, hold, hold!

AUFIDIUS

My noble masters, hear me speak.

1 LORD

O Tullus!

2 LORD

Thou hast done a deed whereat valour will weep.

3 LORD

Tread not upon him. Masters all, be quiet;
Put up your swords.

AUFIDIUS

My lords, when you shall know – as in this rage,
Provok'd by him, you cannot – the great danger
Which this man's life did owe you, you'll rejoice

143–4 ***herald . . . urn*** an Elizabethan rather than Roman custom by which respected men were given a burial procession.

151 ***widowed and unchilded*** Aufidius is careful to mention the effect of Coriolanus' actions on the Volscian women to leave us with the impression of him committing crimes against the innocent rather than being a great soldier. This must be a key image in any consideration of the sincerity of Aufidius' remorse.

That he is thus cut off. Please it your honours
To call me to your Senate, I'll deliver
Myself your loyal servant, or endure
Your heaviest censure.

1 LORD

Bear from hence his body,
And mourn you for him. Let him be regarded
As the most noble corse that ever herald
Did follow to his urn.

2 LORD

His own impatience
Takes from Aufidius a great part of blame.
Let's make the best of it.

AUFIDIUS

My rage is gone,
And I am struck with sorrow. Take him up.
Help, three o' th' chiefest soldiers; I'll be one.
Beat thou the drum, that it speak mournfully;
Trail your steel pikes. Though in this city he
Hath widowed and unchilded many a one,
Which to this hour bewail the injury,
Yet he shall have a noble memory.
Assist.

Exeunt, bearing the body of CORIOLANUS. *A dead march sounded*

Study programme

Before reading the play

Tragedy

Whereas we all understand what is meant by a 'comedy', and have certain expectations when we go to see one, the meaning of the term 'tragedy' has been clouded by its overuse, particularly in the popular press, and so it will mean different things to each of us. For some it is a tragedy when their football team gets beaten; for some a tragedy involves loss of life on a large scale; for others, the term is used to describe the break-up of a relationship. The list could go on and on.

1. What do you understand the word tragedy to mean? Describe three incidents which you would call tragedies.

2. Look out for uses of the word 'tragedy', or derivatives of it, in the media. Does there seem to be any consensus on what the word means and how serious it is?

In theatrical terms, *Tragedy* is concerned with the downfall of a central character. Aristotle produced the first definition of the genre in his book ***Poetics***, taking as his model the plays of Ancient Greece. In his eyes, *the tragic hero* is someone who arouses both our sympathy and terror because although he is in some way better than us, we can see within his character a mixture of good and evil. He has *a tragic flaw*, a personality weakness, causing him to make an error of judgement which brings about his fall from greatness to misery, and ultimately death. As he falls, he recognises his mistake and so gains salvation: he dies with us sympathising with him because we see his misfortune as being greater than he deserves. In his tragedy we also recognise potential for our own and so learn from the experience.

Later tragedians adapted this model somewhat. Sixteenth-century Christian models of the genre tended to put an emphasis upon pride as the tragic flaw, as this was the Cardinal Sin which had led to Man's downfall. Similarly, as thought developed in the seventeenth century, the Elizabethans became interested in the way in which a man's personality, if constant, could lead him into being a victim of circumstances: in other words, he became the victim of the society which had moulded him.

3 One of the difficulties with ***Coriolanus*** is that it does not conform to one of these models but appears to have elements of all three. Whilst you are reading the play look out for and record events which reveal:

- Coriolanus making errors of judgement;
- Coriolanus demonstrating facets of pride;
- Coriolanus as a victim of circumstances and the ideals which have been bred into him.

Look at the lists you have made and decide which is the key event in each category which makes his death inevitable.

Plot

The structure of ***Coriolanus*** would appear at first sight to be straightforward, in that there are no sub-plots to divert our attention from the progress of the central character. However, the play is action-packed, with little time being given to introspection by the characters, so it is important to note down what happens when. The Act summaries will help you to do this but they provide only a very brief commentary on events: you may well want to make more detailed scene summaries of your own as you read the text.

If you are to be able to evaluate the character of Coriolanus fully, you must look closely at the way the play has been structured. In ***Coriolanus: Penguin Critical Studies***, Stephen Coote argues that there are four main phases in the tragedy:

- *the protasis* in which characters are introduced and the principle conflicts established;
- *the epitasis* in which the hero is seen in his full military glory, at the pinnacle of his achievement;
- *the catastasis* in which the hero returns triumphantly and is then rejected;
- *the catastrophe* in which the hero falls and eventually dies.

1 Using this model and the Act summaries, decide which scenes fall into each stage. Look at the character of Coriolanus in each. As a focus for your notes, you should think about the positive and negative characteristics he shows in each stage. This will allow you to understand the nature of his tragedy more.

2 An alternative view of structure would be to look at the play's primary concern as being with politics and so to divide it up in this way. By doing this, you will become aware of an interesting parallel in terms of events – scenes of war and then peace in the Roman state are mirrored in the Volscian state, with Coriolanus being a central figure in both. By looking at the difference between his conduct in foreign and domestic politics, one can get a very clear picture of his limitations as both a politician and a human being.

A favourite device of Shakespeare is the use of *mirrors* and *foils*. The use of mirrors means that certain events are duplicated in order for either key themes to be drawn out or for the actions of key characters to be contrasted. Similarly, the tragic hero will often have one or more characters who are similar to him in situation, and whose reactions to events can therefore be compared with his own: the dramatic term for these is foils.

3 As you are reading the text, look out for events which are replicated. To give you a start, look for scenes in which:

- characters beg – contrast the way they do this and their motives for doing it;
- processions take place – contrast the nature of these.

4 As you read, contrast the actions and motives of Aufidius and Coriolanus.

The theme of politics

If you have read other Shakespearean plays, or have studied Tudor history, you will be aware that the government of England during the dramatist's lifetime was monarchical, with the King or Queen claiming to be God's representative on Earth. Below the monarch was a strict hierarchy of social positions and it was felt that disruption of this by an aspiring person would lead to disruption for all. The two things which could occur because of this – civil strife and foreign invasion – were major fears in England, a country which had relatively recently suffered civil war and which was constantly faced with the threat of invasion from Catholic Spain. Usurpation, and its effect upon social order, was thus a major theme in Elizabethan drama, with a model of organic government, in which each constituent played its part to ensure the health of all, being propounded.

By the time ***Coriolanus*** was written, Shakespeare was beginning to explore more complex forms of politics, and particularly to look at the ways in which a man's personal aspirations and loyalties could clash with his wider duty to the State. Because England provided such a static model, his research led him to look at the situation in Ancient Rome, and particularly the alternative system of government it embodied. It is necessary for you to have a basic knowledge of this before reading the text.

The play is set in the very earliest days of Rome, when the city was struggling to maintain its identity against other rival states in its locality. It had moved from a monarchical system of government to an aristocratic model because its previous rulers had been expelled, charged with being tyrants. As the play opens, the Senate, Rome's noble rulers, are about to begin an experiment in democratisation – they will bow to the demands of an angry mob for representation in government.

The play will thus have as one of its central themes the effect of democratisation on the health of a nation state. Shakespeare's reason for choosing such an era can be understood when one realises that during the year preceding the writing of the play (1607), the Corn Riots had occurred in the West Midlands of England, the dramatist's home.

1 As you are reading the play, think about whether Shakespeare is in favour of democratisation or not. Key factors in this will be his depiction of:

- the citizens – as individuals and as a mob
- the tribunes to the people
- the patricians.

You should also look out for images of the political state as being a living body, and of the diseases which it is subject to.

Whereas most people who have religious faith see their greatest rewards as coming after death, the founding fathers of Rome had decreed that it was a heavenly city on Earth and so the greatest reward its citizens could have would be to be of service to it. At the heart of this belief were two precepts:

- Private loyalties – e.g. to friends and family – should be sacrificed to the public good. This entailed the subordination of instinct and emotional needs to the need to do 'the greater good'.

- The highest honour a man could have was to die for Rome. As Plutarch, Shakespeare's source pointed out,

> ... in those days, valiantness was honoured in Rome above all other virtues.

Shakespeare's interest in this was the strain it placed upon the individual to act in an unnatural way, and the conflict of emotions which could therefore arise if one was faced with a duty to Rome and a duty to oneself or family. He noticed that the cult of bravery was largely designed for times of war, and was thus life-denying, and that it allowed only those capable of military feats to be regarded as virtuous. He was intrigued by the prospect of a man being immersed in these ideals, and so trying to live his life according to them in times of peace, when internal politics might demand a much more flexible approach. He found material to explore these interests in the story of Caius Martius Coriolanus in Plutarch's ***Parallel Lives***.

2 As you read the text, try to find evidence of Coriolanus being a product of his mother's teachings about the duty of a Roman noble. Look at the problems this causes for him.

During reading

Act I

Check your knowledge of Act I

- What do the citizens say is the cause of their riot?
- What reasons do the citizens give for Marcius serving Rome?
- What does Menenius hope to show the rioters in his 'Fable of the Belly'?
- What is Marcius' opinion of the citizens of Rome? Why does he welcome the prospect of war?

- Why do the tribunes think that Marcius can only benefit from his role in the forthcoming war?
- Why has Aufidius decided to attack Rome now?
- How does Marcius capture Corioli?
- Why is Aufidius so annoyed at the soldiers who help him fight Marcius?
- Who does Marcius ask for mercy for and why is this request not carried out?
- Which rewards does Marcius refuse and which does he accept?
- What pledge does Aufidius make regarding Marcius?

Questioning the text in Act I

1 The first scene in the play is a vital one as it introduces the primary political conflict, establishes the personality of two of the lead characters and creates an atmosphere of noisy turmoil which will dominate proceedings henceforth.

- In a small group, attempt to bring the scene to life, creating the atmosphere of an urban riot on stage. As you take your parts, think carefully about what each character is hoping to achieve as he enters the stage, and what his main objective is. This should inform the way you move and speak throughout the scene.
- Remain in role, and, in turn, explain what the political problems in Rome are in the eyes of:
  - the citizens
  - Menenius
  - Marcius.

  What solutions would each propose?
- Out of role, consider what each character has said. What genuine grievances have been aired?

2 Look at the 'Fable of the Belly' which Menenius related (scene 1, lines 93ff.) It compares the political state to a human body, and thus begins a dominant symbol in the play.

Complete the diagram below in order to make sense of the fable:

Part of body	**Function**	**Roman equivalent**	**Function**
Head	to rule through reason		
Heart	to give counsel to the head		
Belly			
Arm			
Leg			
Outer limbs			

Look at the information you gathered in Assignment 1. If the body is the model of an ideal political state, how does Rome measure up to it? In what ways are key parties failing to fulfil their roles?

3 Marcius is dismissive of the people and their complaints and in scene 1, lines 163–185, accuses them of being cowardly, untrustworthy, fickle and potentially self-destructive. Look at their actions in scenes 1, 4 and 5 and decide how much of this diatribe is justified.

4 In scene 3, the audience sees the mother of Marcius for the first time, although her influence over him has already been described by the first citizen. Explain what you think she has brought Marcius up to believe, using her speech at the opening of the scene and her pronouncement that:

The breasts of Hecuba,
When she did suckle Hector, look'd not lovelier
Than Hector's forehead when it spit forth blood
At Grecian sword, contemning.

(lines 43–6)

5 Scenes 4 to 8 are short and hectic because in them the action of a major battle must be captured, a feat which is very difficult to carry off on stage.

In a group of no more than eight, present these scenes in a way which will make them as realistic and dramatic as possible. You should pay particular attention to:

- character groupings;
- the way scenes are linked by movement, and particularly the way characters enter and leave the stage;
- fight scenes, and how these can be choreographed to gain maximum dramatic effect;
- the use of stage effects (e.g. lighting and background noise) to heighten the atmosphere of conflict.

6 Aufidius is intended to be a foil for Marcius, a contrasting personality who will allow us to see the hero in a more sympathetic light. Compare the two as they appear in scenes 2 to 10, paying particular attention to:

- their attitudes to the Senators of their respective countries;
- their attitudes to war, and their reasons for waging it;
- their attitudes to honour, and how this changes in the course of the Act;
- their attitudes to each other, and the reasons for their rivalry;
- how others describe them.

If you were a director, would you want them to come across almost as super-heroes for their countries or as two adolescents playing a game of their own whilst others suffer? How could you convey either of these views to your audience?

7 We see Marcius address his troops in scene 4, lines 23–42 and in scene 6, lines 67–85. Using these speeches, and possibly that of Cominius in scene 6, lines 1–9, describe what you think are his strengths and weaknesses as:

- a soldier
- a leader of men.

8 Within this Act, the following are said of Marcius:

- chief enemy to the people (scene 1, lines 5–6)
- a very dog to the commonalty (scene 1, lines 25–6)
- pays himself with being proud (scene 1, lines 30–1)
- he did it to please his mother (scene 1, line 36)
- What he cannot help in his nature you account a vice in him. You must in no way say he is covetous (scene 1, lines 39–40)
- He is grown/Too proud to be so valiant (scene 1, lines 255–6)
- O noble fellow!
  Who sensibly outdares his senseless sword (scene 4, lines 53–4)
- Flower of warriors (scene 6, line 32)

In addition, the tribunes question his motives for serving under Cominius in scene 1, lines 260–73. In a small group, look carefully at each judgement on Marcius in the light of the way he behaves both in Rome and on the battlefield during this Act.

9 Look again at the quotes listed in Assignment 8. Which do you agree with and which do you think are wrong? Give textual evidence to support your views.

What do you think are Marcius' strengths and weaknesses as:

- a servant of Rome?
- a human being?

10 Three important sets of images develop from the first Act which you need to chart throughout the play.

- The first is relatively simple, in that it concerns the comparisons of people with animals, both real and legendary.
- The second is more complicated because although it could be entitled 'Images of Eating', it also incorporates comparisons of people to foodstuffs, references to cannibalism and to self-devourment.
- The third has its roots in 'The Fable of the Belly' and concerns images of the body and its attendant diseases.

Divide up into groups and each take responsibility for tracking the use of one set of images throughout the play. You should list your findings on a wall chart in a similar way to the following:

Act, scene, line reference	Who?	Is compared to what?	By whom?	Why? (Intended effect of image)

Act 2

Check your knowledge of Act 2

- How do Menenius and the tribunes differ in their views of Coriolanus?
- What ambition does Volumnia have for her son? How does he feel about this?
- How does Coriolanus receive praise?
- Why do the tribunes fear him?
- What reservation does Brutus add to his support of Coriolanus in the Senate?
- What ceremony does Coriolanus ask to be exempted from?
- What reservations do the citizens have about Coriolanus?
- Why do they feel they should vote for him?
- How does Coriolanus see the tradition of begging for votes?
- What do the tribunes advise the people to do after they have promised Coriolanus their votes?

Questioning the text in Act 2

1 Just as our attention was focused upon Coriolanus in the first Act, so his enemies, the tribunes, come into focus in this one. Menenius tells them:

> I know you can do very little alone; for your helps
> are many, or else your actions would grow
> wondrous single: your abilities are too infant-like
> for doing much alone. You talk of pride. O that
> you could turn your eyes toward the napes of
> your necks, and make an interior survey of
> your good selves!

(scene 1, lines 34–40)

If you were directing Sicinius or Brutus on stage, would you adhere to this description, and thus make them the villains of the piece, or would you present them in a more favourable light? To help you make your decision, look at the following in this Act:

- the accusations they make against Coriolanus (e.g. scene 1, lines 207–72) and whether these are justified;
- their motives for opposing Coriolanus;
- the way they speak to and manipulate the people in scene 3.

2 In a play which is about politics, much attention must be given to rhetoric: the way people use language to influence others. In scene 3 of this Act, the tribunes persuade the people to take back their approval of Coriolanus' election. In pairs, imagine you are the actors who have been given the parts of the tribunes in this scene. Look carefully at lines 152–255.

- Identify the ways in which they use rhetorical questions to influence their audience.
- Look at other linguistic tricks they employ to meet their aims and think about where you will put emphasis when reading the lines aloud.
- Decide what tone you will use with your audience: will you scold, be sympathetic or sarcastic with them? Will you both use the same tone or will you each take a different tack?
- Decide what gestures and facial expressions you will use, and how you will move or stand when giving the speeches.
- Decide whether you will address just the mob on stage or include the whole theatre audience in your appeal. How could you do the latter and what would be your motives for so doing?
- Take turns acting out the scene to your class and comment on how effective each performance was.

In doing this, try to isolate the things which make language and non-verbal gestures persuasive.

3 Menenius is the arch-politician in the play, and is thus difficult to pin down as a character. In groups, look at how he behaves in Acts 1 and 2, as well as what is said about him, by both himself and others, and decide:

- what is his opinion of the people and their grievances;
- what he thinks of Coriolanus;
- why he has been described by one actor as 'someone who will survive no matter what happens'.

4 A crucial step in the life of Coriolanus is to try to become consul, the supreme political office in Rome. Initially he is reluctant to undertake this, yet by the end of the Act he has won the people's vote.

- Who and what are the key factors in his decision to stand for the office? What motives do people have for persuading him to do this?
- How suitable is he to be consul? Think about his attitude to the people whom he will govern; his political skills, or lack of them; his attitude to the constitution of Rome; his services for his country.

5 A theme which is developed in this Act, and which you will need to track, is that of ingratitude. A number of characters express different views on what should be given to Coriolanus as a reward for his services but the issue is made more complicated by the attitude of the hero. Because he sees valour as a prize in itself, he wants no other recognition than to serve Rome on the battlefield, yet he expects to be elected consul without having to go through the motions of a popular vote.

To make sense of this, you need to look throughout the play for occasions where characters speak of 'service', the rewards they expect for this, and how they respond to what they perceive to be ingratitude. Chart such occasions in the manner below:

Reference	Character	Quotation	Attitude shown

6 An important image begun in this Act is that of 'acting', one which Coriolanus in particular uses when he feels he is behaving in an unnatural way. Trace the occasions when he does this and notice what it shows about his views on natural and unnatural ways to act. This will allow you to judge whether he is a balanced human being and to have a clearer understanding of his motives for acting in the way he does.

Act 3

Check your knowledge of Act 3

- Where are Coriolanus and Menenius going as the Act begins? What are they discussing?
- What does Coriolanus think of the people having the power to affect political decisions?
- Why is he guilty of treason?
- What is the consequence of the ædiles attempt to arrest him? How do the nobles react:
  - during this affray?
  - after it?
- What animal do the tribunes compare Coriolanus to? Is the comparison a fitting one?

- What does Volumnia tell him he must do?
- Which accusation, made by Volumnia, succeeds in getting him to change his mind?
- What crime do the tribunes accuse Coriolanus of?
- What punishments are possible for treason? Which one is passed on Coriolanus?
- What consequence, arising from his punishment, does Coriolanus prophesy for Rome?

Questioning the test in Act 3

1. In Act 3, scene 1, Coriolanus states very clearly why he opposes the democratisation of Rome. List his arguments as accurately as you can, stating whether, given the events in the play up to the end of this Act, he is justified in his fears. Look closely at the language he uses in stating his views and the solution he comes up with to the political problem. This will help you to see his limitations as a politician.

2. In Act 3, scene 1, lines 33–6, the people are once more compared to mouths, and more specifically voices, an image which recurs throughout the play. Why is it an appropriate one to use?

3. Look carefully at the way in which the nobility speak *of* and *to* the people in this Act. What are the crucial differences between them and Coriolanus? Does this comparison enable the hero to be seen in a more or less favourable light? Explain your views.

4. Imagine you are Coriolanus in Act 3, scene 2, listening to those you hold most dear betray everything you believe in. Write an interior monologue which will capture your thoughts and feelings as this scene progresses. You should cover the following areas:
   - what you are feeling as the scene begins;

- your mother's silence and how you react to this;
- what arguments your mother then puts forward and how you feel about these. Is she letting you down?
- why you finally agree to do something which you feel is wrong;
- what you think about the way you must act and its potential effect upon you;
- what you feel about yourself, your friends and Rome as you leave for the market place.

5 In scene 3, Brutus says,

> Put him to choler straight. He hath been us'd
> Ever to conquer, and to have his worth
> Of contradiction; being once chaf'd, he cannot
> Be rein'd again to temperance; then he speaks
> What's in his heart, and that is there which looks
> With us to break his neck.
>
> (lines 25–30)

In a small group, look carefully at the whole of this scene, act it out and then decide whether Coriolanus falls due to his own character, the machinations of the tribunes, or a mixture of both, as this quotation suggests.

You will need to consider such things as:

- the behaviour of Coriolanus in Act I, scene I and the sentiments he expresses in Act 2, scene 3;
- his readiness to use force against the mob in Act 3, scene I;
- his inner conflict in Act 3, scene 2;
- his behaviour throughout this scene;
- the way the tribunes speak to the mob in Act 2, scene 3;
- their initial meeting with the senators in this Act and their intent within it;

- their actions as unrest breaks out at the end of scene 1;
- their preparations at the beginning of Act 3, scene 3, and what it shows about the way they work;
- the way they use language to both make the citizens aware of old grievances and to taunt Coriolanus.

6 At the end of this scene, do you regard the exile of Coriolanus as:

- the necessary removal of a potential tyrant?
- a shameful act of ingratitude which will damage the state of Rome?

Justify your view, using the text as evidence.

7 Imagine you are Cominius completing a diary entry on the events of the day. Give a full account not only of what happened, but what you feel was the importance of the events and why the Senate allowed Coriolanus to be exiled after all he had done for Rome.

Act 4

Check your knowledge of Act 4

- In his farewell to his family, where does Coriolanus say he will go? What animal does he compare himself to?
- How do the tribunes decide to act after he is banished? Why?
- What information does Nicanor give to the Volscian spy?
- Where does Coriolanus go and how is he received?
- What does he resolve to do and how does Aufidius pledge to help him?
- How has Rome been affected by the banishment of Coriolanus?

- When news comes of the alliance between Aufidius and Coriolanus, what is the reaction of:
  - the tribunes
  - Menenius
  - the citizens?
- In what way does Coriolanus anger Aufidius?
- What three potential reasons does Aufidius see to explain the fall of Coriolanus in Rome?
- What prediction does he make about Coriolanus?

Questioning the text in Act 4

1 In the first scene of this Act, we see a change in the character of Coriolanus. What is this and what is its intended impact upon the audience?

2 Scene 4 is quite often cut from productions as directors feel it brings little new to the play. If you were directing the play, would you cut or keep the scene? Justify your decision by showing the improvement your decision would bring to the play.

3 In scene 4, Coriolanus enters the house of his old enemy as the result of what could seem to us an incomprehensible decision. Imagine you are him and explain to your audience what has brought you to Antium. Use all of the scene, as well as what you know of his character already, in order to help you, but look particularly at lines 12–26 for clues.

4 In scene 5, Aufidius embraces Coriolanus, using some of the most poetic language of the play. This is a potentially difficult scene to carry off and in previous productions it has been interpreted as:

- showing a soldier's love for one who he admires;

- revealing a homo-erotic attraction between the two men;
- showing a narcissism on the part of both: they admire each other as mirror images of themselves;
- as further evidence of Aufidius' potential for treachery – his profession of love is insincere;
- as the meeting of two traitors, who owe no allegiance to anything but themselves;
- as sincere – now that Aufidius has Coriolanus at his mercy, he can love him.

How do you think Shakespeare intended this meeting to be perceived by his audience?

Try acting out the scene in accordance with the different interpretations. Which work best?

5 In scene 6, we see the tribunes triumphant in a peaceful Rome. What is the dramatic impact of placing this scene *after* the one in which Coriolanus and Aufidius are reconciled?

6 Look at Menenius' behaviour to the tribunes before the news comes of the Volscian attack, and of he and Cominius immediately after. Does this shed light upon why Rome has faced an internal political crisis? Does it add justification to Coriolanus' denunciation of all Romans in scene 5, lines 64–100?

7 In scene 7, Aufidius once more determines to destroy Coriolanus. If you were taking the part, would you play this scene in a naturalistic way, as showing the feelings of a man who has been betrayed and so has a genuine grievance; or would you represent him more as a stage/pantomime villain? How would your decision affect the reading of his final speech?

Act 5

Check your knowledge of Act 5

- As the scene begins, where is Coriolanus and how has he got there so swiftly? (You need to look at Act 4, too).
- How was Cominius' suit for mercy received?
- Why does Menenius feel he will be more successful? How is he received?
- Volumnia tries in many ways to convince Coriolanus to be merciful. How does she succeed?
- How does Coriolanus signal his acceptance of her proposal?
- What does he predict for himself?
- What is the consequence of the siege on the tribunes?
- What does Aufidius accuse Coriolanus of?
- How does Coriolanus die?
- What does Aufidius do
  - immediately after Coriolanus is slaughtered?
  - when he has been chided by the Volscian nobles?

Questioning the text in Act 5

1 The character of Menenius is one which has caused much debate and in this Act, in particular, his motives are open to question. Imagine you are playing the character in the first two scenes of this Act. Look back at your previous notes upon his preoccupations and behaviour, and decide what these scenes add to our understanding of his personality. Is his initial refusal sincere or is he merely making the tribunes squirm? Does he accept the mission because he has been flattered or does he have the safety of Rome at heart? Is he a falsely arrogant old fool or a wily old fox? Does he really 'know' Coriolanus? What is the effect upon him, if any, of being sent away?

It may help you to look at a potential foil for him, Cominius.

2 Scene 3 is crucial to our understanding of Coriolanus and, potentially, to his understanding of himself. In lines 34–7, he says he is determined that he will,

> … never
> Be such a gosling to obey instinct, but stand
> As if a man were author of himself
> And knew no other kin.

Look at the way in which he struggles to suppress the emotions he is feeling inside as his family plead for mercy.

- Identify ways in which the language shows that Coriolanus is in turmoil. Look in particular for times when an uncharacteristic extravagance in the way he speaks betrays emotion bubbling through.
- Analyse what the scene adds to our feelings for him, given that his dismissal of Cominius and Menenius has seemed so cold.
- Look carefully at lines 186–99:
  - does this acceptance of his fate add to his noble stature?
  - has he learned something in the scene?
- Decide how he will behave as the scene unfolds – will he be the 'boy of tears' which Aufidius will later call him or will he possess a greater dignity? How would you convey either of these interpretations in your reading of the text?

3 Scene 3 has two moments which, although subdued, could hold great dramatic intensity. If you were directing the piece:

- how long would you hold the silence between Coriolanus and his mother following line 182? What is it intended to convey?
- how would you get Aufidius to deliver line 194? Justify your decision.

4 Using your answers to Assignment 2, how do you interpret the behaviour of Coriolanus in scene 6? Is it one final attempt to avoid defeat or is he prepared to die?

5 Scene 6 is one of the many episodes in the play where Shakespeare mirrors previous events. Contrast the scene with the expulsion of Coriolanus from Rome in order to get a clearer picture of Aufidius, the tribunes, the mob, the nobles and the hero. How does this raise the status of Coriolanus?

6 Who triumphs at the end: Aufidius? Coriolanus? His family? The Volscians? Rome? The people? No one?

As a group, explore different interpretations and decide which most suits Shakespeare's intention.

After reading

Plot

Shakespeare's use of his source

Shakespeare's only source for the storyline of the play was Plutarch's ***Parallel Lives*** – try to read the chapter about Coriolanus if you can. In writing his own play, however, he did alter the story in the following ways:

- events were telescoped into a few weeks;
- events were re-ordered, with Menenius, Volumnia and the riots being introduced at the beginning not half way through;
- the character of Menenius was expanded beyond being a representative of the Senate into having a paternal relationship with Coriolanus;
- the unnamed foe of Coriolanus in the first battle became Aufidius, his personal rival and foil;

- Volumnia was expanded into being a Roman matriach, with much power over her son;
- Cominius was pictured as a friend of Coriolanus' family;
- the tribunes were shown to be rejected by the people at the end;
- the cause of the riots was changed from being about usury and corn to just being about corn;
- the dramatist made Coriolanus enter Corioli alone rather than with a few men;
- scenes in which Coriolanus was welcomed home by the citizens and accepted as consul by the Senate were added;
- In Plutarch, Marcius keeps the spoils he won in Antium and, when refused the consulship, tries to abolish the post of tribune and stop the distribution of corn.

1 In role as Shakespeare, explain what you hoped to achieve, in terms of dramatic impact, by each of these changes.

Shakespeare's use of irony

The play is rich in *irony*, a device the effect of which depends upon the audience having an insight into events which a character lacks. This can lead to them saying inappropriate things, to unwittingly predicting the future accurately or hopelessly inaccurately.

In ***Coriolanus***, Shakespeare achieves an ironical effect in two ways. The first, a commonly used device, is to have characters say things which will gain relevance later in the text. In Act 4, when Aufidius readily accepts Coriolanus into his house and gives him half his command, the audience remember his oath in Act 1, that he will kill the latter even if it means breaking the laws of hospitality. Thus the past offers a chilling sense of foreboding upon the events which the audience is watching.

1 Trace other speeches in the play in which this device is used and say what it brings to our understanding of character and action on those occasions.

The second device lies in the way the plot is structured, and particularly the way in which the scenes are ordered. Consistently the audience sees an event and then hears those who have not been present at it predict its outcome, usually in a hopelessly incorrect way.

2 The following are examples of this. What effect do they have upon the audience?

- In Act 3, scene 1, the senators make their way to the market place to have the election of Coriolanus formally ratified, unaware of the events at the end of Act 2.
- In Act 4, scene 6, the tribunes celebrate their victory, unaware of the alliance between Coriolanus and Aufidius agreed upon in scene 5.
- In Act 4, scene 6, Menenius denies that Coriolanus could ever ally with Aufidius.
- In Act 5, scene 4, Menenius derides the notion that Volumnia will win over Coriolanus, unaware that she has already done so.

3 Are there other examples of this device in the play? If so, what are they and what effect do they have?

Themes

Coriolanus is one of Shakespeare's most political plays, one in which he explores both the debasing nature of politics and the effect which wider responsibilities can have upon a man's more intimate needs. In the Introduction, the tension between the hero's need to serve his country and his bond to his mother was indicated. Having read the play and completed the Assignments for each Act, you should now be in a position to appreciate this much more. Shakespeare is using it to show that the very thing which made Rome great – the cult of honour – was the weakness which would destroy it, because it demanded that men ignore their natural ties.

1 Ensure that you have full notes on the way this and the theme of ingratitude are developed in the play.

A related theme, and one rarely picked up by commentators, is the transience of human achievement. In Act 4, scene 7, Aufidius comments:

> So our virtues
> Lie in th' interpretation of the time;
> And power, unto itself most commendable,
> Hath not a tomb so evident as a chair
> T' extol what it hath done.
>
> (lines 49–53)

2 Such a revelation is interesting coming from one so steeped in envy, and says much about his character, but what does it also tell us about:

- the hero and his pursuit of valour? Does it diminish him?
- our own lives?

Is its effect to give the play an anti-war slant or are we not to take it too seriously? To help you to make a decision, look at the ways in which

- war is pictured as both a game and as an endless massacre;
- Aufidius' words are echoed, or contradicted, by others.

Characters

In a workshop on the play, the actor, Philip Voss, described how he prepares for a part. Using guidelines laid down by the dramatic theorist, Stanislavsky, he begins by reading the play, making notes of:

- all clear facts about the character;
- what is said about him by others;
- what he says about others and himself.

He then looks at these notes and draws conclusions about what the character's main objective is throughout the play, and how this informs his actions. Having established this, he looks at how it affects the way the character dresses, moves, speaks and responds to others. He then explains his interpretation to other members of the cast and to the director, in order for debate to refine it. Although this is a lengthy process, it may well be one that you could follow for each of the characters in the play.

The following section is intended to enable you to look at different interpretations of the characters and to judge for yourself how you think they should be presented on stage.

Coriolanus

1 In Act 4, scene 7, lines 35–49 Aufidius, in one of the most impartial speeches in the play, dissects the fall of Coriolanus. As a group, look carefully at the speech and at the statements below made about the nature of Coriolanus' tragedy by a group of A-level students:

- 'His problem is that he is too noble; he will not say anything that he does not believe.'
- 'He is an overgrown boy hiding in a suit of armour.'

- 'His tragedy is that he has outlived his usefulness: he is outdated in Rome.'
- 'He is a victim not of the mob but of his mother.'
- 'He is too good to survive in a world of lies and deceit.'
- 'He is arrogant and destructive: it is the people who are the victims, not him.'
- 'He cares only for himself, not for others, and so cannot fit into society.'
- 'His tragedy is that he hates the people so much.'
- 'His tragedy is that he has believed all the myths about Rome.'

Which of these do you agree with? Do you feel that some of his perceived weaknesses are in fact strengths? Can you isolate a weakness which makes his death inevitable? If so, trace the course of his downfall and inevitable death, showing how it is responsible for the actions he undertakes.

2 Coriolanus is accused throughout the play of being proud yet he constantly refuses praise or rewards. Imagine you are a psychiatrist analysing this facet of his character in order to see whether the accusations are valid and whether this is indeed a personality defect. Write a report, in which you analyse manifestations of pride in him as:

- a soldier for Rome;
- a noble in Rome;
- a soldier for the Volsces.

What are the reasons for his pride? How is it shown? Is he guilty of narcissism or is there more to it than that? Quote evidence from the text to support your views.

Volumnia

Volumnia has a key influence upon the life of Coriolanus, yet critics debate whether this is healthy or destructive. Those who see her as a Roman matriach, hungry for honour forbidden to women and so living her life through her son, point out that she never mentions her husband but instead centres her existence upon her offspring. They feel that her readiness to sacrifice him to the pursuit of honour makes her a cold mother, one who demands that her love be earned rather than giving it freely. Thus they feel that Coriolanus' lack of humanity can be traced back to the way she has nurtured him and see her ambition for political office as being the key to his downfall: she pushes him into pursuing an office which he is singly unfit for.

To others, she is the natural product of a city whose code demands personal sacrifice, and thus is herself a victim of the system. This school of belief pictures, her anticipation of Coriolanus' return from Corioli as showing the natural anxiety of a mother whose son is at war, and her reception of him as indicative of huge relief. They feel that her attempt to get him to be more temperate is a desperate attempt to save his life and that her meeting with the tribunes after his banishment shows her real pain.

3 Imagine you are writing the director's notes for the actress who is to take the part of Volumnia. Decide which interpretation of the character she is to adhere to and then write a detailed account of how this is to be illustrated by her performance in Act 1, scene 3; Act 2, scene 1; Act 3, scene 2; Act 5, scene 3 and Act 5, scene 5. If you wish, you may concentrate upon key speeches within these Acts and analyse how the actress should move and speak as she says them.

Virgilia

Students sometimes complain about being given the part of Virgilia, claiming that it is boring because the character never says anything.

Indeed Coriolanus, himself, refers to her as, 'My gracious silence' (Act 2, scene 1, line 177). However, to dismiss her would be to ignore the role she plays as Volumnia's foil and the humane responses she constantly evokes from her husband. Indeed, the fact that he has chosen her as a wife gives us an insight into his character.

4 Look carefully at the scenes in which Virgilia is present and analyse what she brings to them. Would it be correct to say that she is an effective symbol of the suffering war brings to women (e.g. the play makes constant reference to 'rape' and 'widowing' as consequences of war)? What would be lost by her omission?

Menenius

In the Royal Shakespeare Company's 1995 production of ***Coriolanus***, Menenius came across as the only character with whom the audience could really sympathise. The actor, Philip Voss, in discussion of his role, said that he believed the main priority for the patrician was to ensure the safety of Rome and that he saw the election of Marcius as consul as crucial to this. He pictured the senator as a leopard, mixing nobility with stealth, and stressed how able he was to mix with both the people and his peers. An important facet of the character was, for Voss, his love for Coriolanus, and he saw him as heartbroken by his rejection at the end. He accepted that, in many respects, Menenius was a voluptuary but felt that this added to his charm.

An alternative view of Menenius is that he is a time-server, a man of words who survives because he has few principles and is prepared to go with the popular mood. He champions Coriolanus because the warrior possesses the very qualities he lacks, and thus is guilty of naive hero-worship. Even in Rome's darkest hour, his instinct is to pursue old scores and to promote his own ego.

5 Obviously the interpretation of such a major character will have an important effect on the way the play as a whole is presented. Look carefully at the two character portraits of Menenius above and analyse the impact each would have on the way we see the character of Coriolanus. Decide which one you think is most akin to Shakespeare's intention and, with reference to the text, defend your view in a class debate upon Menenius.

The people and their tribunes

It is hard for those of us who have been brought up with a tradition of democratic rights and trade unionism not to sympathise with the plight of the people but we should be wary of forcing our principles upon the play.

6 In order to perceive Shakespeare's view, and thus to decide whether the proletariat are the villains or victims of the piece, look at:

- the way the people are perceived as individuals (Act 1, scene 1, lines 12–22; Act 2, scene 2, lines 1–37; Act 2, scene 3, lines 1–50), and as a mob;
- the way their tribunes act, and their motives for so doing.

Would it be true to say that the dramatist has sympathy with the people until they reach for political power?

Language

Rhetoric

Only Coriolanus distrusts the power of language to get what he wants, relying instead upon physical force, and it would be true to say that his reticence contrasts with the loquaciousness of the other major characters. Indeed, in many respects, he is the victim of words. He is goaded by the accusation of being a 'traitor' in Rome and a 'boy of tears' in Corioli into the outbursts which lead to his downfall and death, and is persuaded by the rhetoric of Volumnia into courses of action which are fatal to him. Because the play is a political one, in which characters do constantly resort to rhetoric to achieve their ends, you need to look at the conventions used and the effects which they achieve.

The play is full of *antithesis*, the term given to sentences which have a balance of opposites within them. For example, in the opening scene, the first citizen explains the cause of the riot by asking his fellows, 'You are all resolv'd to die than to famish?' (line 3). Here the value of the device in contrasting two courses of action or situations is revealed.

Another device which is commonly used in the play is the *rhetorical question*, the term given to a question which is asked purely for effect and therefore requires no answer. The first thing we hear Sicinius say is, 'Was ever a man so proud as is this Marcius?' (Act I, scene I, line 249), not because he expects a reply from Brutus but because he is expressing a cause for disliking the hero which they both share.

1 In order to get accustomed to these conventions, and to be able to see why they are used, pick out five quotations in which they are employed and explain what their intended effect is.

Public speaking and private thoughts

The play is set in the public arena, with characters getting very little time alone, and this has an impact in the way language is used.

'The Fable of the Belly', which Menenius relates, begins the trend for characters to speak in moral proverbs, delivering the kind of folk wisdom which requires little real thought. Thus in the crucial scene in which Volumnia advises Coriolanus to go back to face the mob with humility, she tells him,

Action is eloquence, and the eyes of th' ignorant
More learned than the ears

(Act 3, scene 2, lines 76–7)

Later he will comfort her, as he faces exile, with the words:

You were us'd
To say extremities was the trier of spirits;
That common chances common men could
bear;

(Act 4, scene1, lines 3–5)

Similarly, because the play is so public, there is little introspection and so the device of the *soliloquy*, whereby a character voices his thoughts aloud, is all but ignored. In its place, we have occasions in which characters appear to become lost in their own thoughts whilst in conversation with others or in public situations. An example of this can be seen in Act 2, scene 3, lines 113–125, in which Marcius, whilst canvassing for votes, gives an insight into his views upon the tradition. Other occasions are when Aufidius analyses the character of Coriolanus, and when the hero himself responds to the embassy of his family.

2 What impression of Rome does this tendency for public rather than private speech give us? How does this fit with the theme of politics, and its encroachment upon public life which we have explored earlier?

Imagery

You should have already made notes on two threads of imagery: that of nourishment and of animalism. An important thread which you should now trace concerns only the major character, and is associated with his development in the course of the play. In Act I, Marcius pictures himself as a 'reaper' who would cut down the 'musty chaff' of the proletariat, and so begins the association of himself with death.

The next image is a visual one, in that Coriolanus appears as a 'thing of blood' as he leaves Corioli, smeared from the wounds of his enemy as well as his own. By Act 2, he is a god; by Act 3, a disease and a viper 'that would depopulate the city and be every man himself'; and by Act 4, 'a fire' which will purge Rome. Most importantly, in Act 5, he is pictured not only as a deity but as 'an engine', 'a kind of nothing' before submitting to his mother and becoming nothing more destructive than 'a boy of tears'.

3 Obviously this set of images gives us our biggest clue as to the way the dramatist wanted the actions of his hero to be perceived. Trace it very carefully, identifying who uses each image, what they intend it to show and its effect upon the audience. The visuality of the motif will allow you, if you wish, to represent this partly in pictures on a wallchart, giving you a striking illustration not only of the destructive power of Coriolanus but also of the awe he is held in by all.

In performance

Nothing can allow you to feel the dramatic force of a play more effectively than actually staging it, and being faced with the decisions which actors and directors must face. The following activities involve decisions which every theatre company would have to make before putting the play on.

A question of motives

1 ***Coriolanus*** is a strange play as on several occasions characters act in a way which leaves their motives open to question: the audience is left to interpret these actions rather than have them explained.

Imagine you are a theatre company about to put on the play. In order for your characters to be fully realised, you need to understand everything they do. Discuss, and come to an agreement about, the following:

- Why do the tribunes accuse Coriolanus of tyranny when they have already convicted him of treason?
- Why do the tribunes exile Coriolanus when they could have him put to death?
- Why does he go to Antium to seek out Aufidius?
- Why does he decide to include the nobles and his family in his revenge?
- Why does Aufidius welcome him into his house?
- Why does Coriolanus decide to spare Rome?
- Why does he then return with Aufidius?
- How do the women behave as they re-enter Rome?

A question of interpretations

2 It is possible to interpret the play in a number of ways and this will affect not only the way in which characters are presented but also, perhaps, your set and costumes. Look at the following interpretations which have been put on the play in modern times and the effect they have had on productions:

- Traditionalists would see the play as a heroic tragedy, one in which a great man falls because of a flaw in his nature. They would, therefore, set it in Ancient Rome. In 1950 an American company took a similar view when they updated the play by setting it in Italy during the Allied invasion of the Second World War. In this the Volscians were dressed as Nazis, the Romans became the people of Italy and Coriolanus was depicted as General Patton.
- The Nazi Party promoted the play in schools in Germany during the 1930s, in the belief that it taught the martial values which Hitler and the Third Reich embodied. Had the hero not fallen, they would undoubtedly have updated the dress to fit in with this view.
- An anti-heroic interpretation would see Marcius as an

overgrown child, emotionally tied to his mother and narcissistic.

- Similarly, left-wing critics see the play as idealising the tribunes as ordinary people who overcome a potential dictator. Directors could achieve this effect by costuming the play in Revolutionary France. In America, it was done by making the people dress like the Nicaraguan Sandinistas whilst Coriolanus became Colonel Oliver North.

Which of these interpretations would you adhere to in your production?

Decide which period you would set the play in and create designs for the set and costumes which you would use.

Omissions

3 Often directors are under pressure of time to cut scenes but there is very little in ***Coriolanus*** which does not concern the central plot. However, in the spy scene, Act 2, scene 2, lines 1–37 and in Act 4, scene 5, lines 147–233, the play is slowed by servants commenting upon its action, almost as an unofficial chorus. Would you cut these scenes or do they have dramatic value?

Study questions

Many of the activities you have already completed in the Study programme will help you to answer the questions which come at the end of this section and many others that you might meet in examinations or as titles for coursework assignments. Before you begin work on them, consider the following points about essay writing.

- The length and detail needed for your essay will depend to some extent upon the conditions under which it is written. These might be:

(a) as an assignment for coursework;
(b) as an answer in an open book examination;
(c) as an answer in an examination where texts are not permitted.

- In the case of (a), you will usually be expected to write at a reasonable length (although there will almost always be a word limit) and you will have sufficient time to research your points and explore them in considerable detail within your essay. Drafting, redrafting and proof-reading are all possible within the time given, and are desirable. Dictionaries, thesauruses and other reference works will all be of use to you.

- In the case of (b), your time for writing will be restricted (work out how long you will have for each question *before* you go into the examination), but you will be able to take in a copy of the text. According to your board's regulations this might either be unmarked or annotated by yourself – CHECK THE REGULATIONS. It may seem a boon to have a text with you, but beware. Spending time flicking desperately through the text in search of quotations or references will always reduce the time available for writing (and thinking). You must make sure that you are very familiar with the text to take advantage of the book on your desk. Do not be tempted to put in quotations for quotations' sake: first ask yourself whether they are necessary and relevant.

- In the case of (c), again your writing time is restricted and you will need to rely entirely on your memory of the text. For both (c) and (b), it is essential to use time effectively, but do *not* miss out the planning stage, and keep a piece of scrap paper handy to jot down ideas as they occur to you. Do not overrun your allocated time – it is often better to write less on, say, all four questions, than to write well on three but lose all marks for the fourth by not attempting it. If this means ending some questions in note form, this is usually acceptable to examiners, provided that your notes are clear and conclusive. Again, CHECK THE

REGULATIONS and ask your teacher's or tutor's advice before the exam.

- In all cases you should read the question carefully. If it includes a quotation, do not ignore it – use it in some way. Remember that you do not have to agree with the statement in a title; you may have a strong argument against it and this will help you. If a title falls into several parts, break it up and deal with each part separately.
- Plan, noting down the ideas you wish to develop and any references or quotations also relevant to the answer.
- Decide on a structure – it may be useful to think of a shape for your argument, perhaps in flow-chart form.

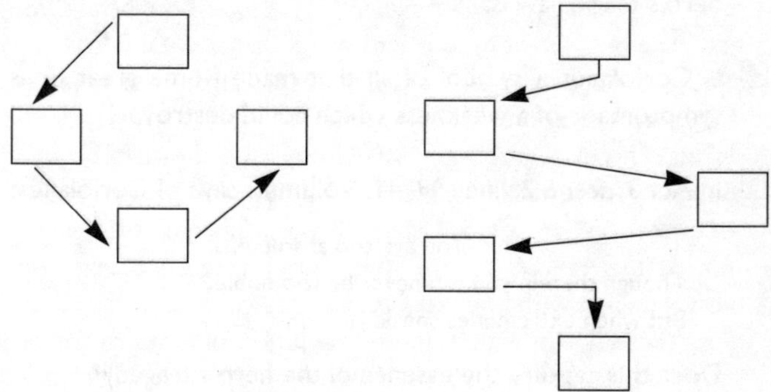

- Organise your notes and references into relevant sections (perhaps keeping to these for your paragraph divisions as you write) and consider how you will link each section to the next.
- Write, starting with a clear introduction setting out your approach or how you intend to tackle the question. Place the bulk of your arguments in the middle of the essay. The conclusion is vital – add any further brief comments and refer back to the title. This will act as a check as to whether you have actually done what you set out to do.

The questions below may be used as coursework assignment titles or serve as revision essays.

1. '***Coriolanus*** is a play which glorifies war!'
   '***Coriolanus*** has an anti-war theme!'
   Which judgement of the play is right?

2. Keats believed that at the heart of the play was the belief that 'one murder makes a villain, millions make a hero.' Do you agree?

3. 'The striking thing about Coriolanus is the amount that he does "alone" and this inability to get on with others is central to his fall.' Discuss this statement, giving your own view of what the hero's tragic flaw is.

4. Is Coriolanus a symbol of all that made Rome great or is he symptomatic of a weakness which could destroy it?

5. In Act 3, scene 2, lines 39–41, Volumnia says of Coriolanus:

   'You are too absolute;
   Though therein you can never be too noble
   But when extremeties speak.'

   Does this capture the essence of the hero's tragedy?

6. Coriolanus calls Sicinius a 'Triton of the minnows'. Does the play as a whole support this derisory judgement of the tribunes?

7. 'The tribunes are essentially the same character split in two. They are inseparable because they are incapable of undertaking any task alone'. Examine the characters of the tribunes in the light of this statement.

8 'The people have a valid grievance yet lose our sympathy as soon as they seek political power.' Do you agree?

9 Is Volumnia a cold, ruthlessly ambitious matriach or a loving mother?

10 'Virgilia says little yet her impact is enormous.' Discuss this view, explaining what the character brings to the play.

11 'Menenius is a survivor precisely because, unlike everyone else in Rome, he has no principles: his first and last concern is always for himself.'
'Menenius holds our sympathy throughout because he is human enough for us to like, wise enough for us to admire.'
Consider these views of the character, showing his dramatic importance to the play.

12 'The real triumph of Coriolanus is that he is able to submit to his mother's plea.' Discuss.

13 'Aufidius becomes less realistic as the play progresses, ending almost as a pantomine villain for us to jeer at.' Discuss this view of Aufidius, showing his importance to the play and commenting on how effective you find him as a character.

14 'The images of death and disease which surround Coriolanus help us to understand his character.' Discuss this statement, showing the importance of the images to the play.

15 '***Coriolanus*** is a play which demonstrates that there is no room for honour in a world where politics dominate.' Discuss.

16 '***Coriolanus*** is a finely crafted piece, in which structure plays a vital part in our understanding of events.' Discuss.

Addison Wesley Longman Limited
Edinburgh Gate, Harlow,
Essex CM20 2JE, England
and Associated Companies throughout the world.

This educational edition first published 1996

Editorial material set in 10/12 point Gill Sans
Produced by Longman Singapore Publishers (Pte) Ltd
Printed in Singapore

ISBN 0 582 28726 X

Cover illustration by Reg Cartwright

The publisher's policy is to use paper manufactured from sustainable forests.

Consultant: Geoff Barton

Longman Literature
Series editor: Roy Blatchford

Novels

Jane Austen ***Pride and Prejudice*** 0 582 07720 6
Charlotte Brontë ***Jane Eyre*** 0 582 07719 2
Emily Brontë ***Wuthering Heights*** 0 582 07782 6
Anita Brookner ***Hotel du Lac*** 0 582 25406 X
Marjorie Darke ***A Question of Courage*** 0 582 25395 0
Charles Dickens ***A Christmas Carol*** 0 582 23664 9
Great Expectations 0 582 07783 4
Hard Times 0 582 25407 8
Oliver Twist 0 582 28729 4
George Eliot ***Silas Marner*** 0 582 23662 2
Anne Fine ***Flour Babies*** 0 582 29259 X
Goggle-Eyes 0 582 29260 3
Madame Doubtfire 0 582 29261 1
F Scott Fitzgerald ***The Great Gatsby*** 0 582 06023 0
Tender is the Night 0 582 09716 9
Nadine Gordimer ***July's People*** 0 582 06011 7
Graham Greene ***The Captain and the Enemy*** 0 582 06024 9
Thomas Hardy ***Far from the Madding Crowd*** 0 582 07788 5
The Mayor of Casterbridge 0 582 22586 8
Tess of the d'Urbervilles 0 582 09715 0
Susan Hill ***The Mist in the Mirror*** 0 582 25399 3
Aldous Huxley ***Brave New World*** 0 582 06016 8
Robin Jenkins ***The Cone-Gatherers*** 0 582 06017 6
Doris Lessing ***The Fifth Child*** 0 582 06021 4
Joan Lindsay ***Picnic at Hanging Rock*** 0 582 08174 2
Bernard Mac Laverty ***Lamb*** 0 582 06557 7
Jan Mark ***The Hillingdon Fox*** 0 582 25985 1
Dalene Matthee ***Fiela's Child*** 0 582 28732 4
Brian Moore ***Lies of Silence*** 0 582 08170 X
Beverley Naidoo ***Chain of Fire*** 0 582 25403 5
Journey to Jo'burg 0 582 25402 7
George Orwell ***Animal Farm*** 0 582 06010 9
Alan Paton ***Cry, the Beloved Country*** 0 582 07787 7
Ruth Prawer Jhabvala ***Heat and Dust*** 0 582 25398 5
Paul Scott ***Staying On*** 0 582 07718 4
Virginia Woolf ***To the Lighthouse*** 0 582 09714 2

Short stories

Jeffrey Archer ***A Twist in the Tale*** 0 582 06022 2
Thomas Hardy ***The Wessex Tales*** 0 582 25405 1
Susan Hill ***A Bit of Singing and Dancing*** 0 582 09711 8
George Layton ***A Northern Childhood*** 0 582 25404 3
Bernard Mac Laverty ***The Bernard Mac Laverty Collection*** 0 582 08172 6
Angelou, Goodison, Senior & Walker ***A Quartet of Stories*** 0 582 28730 8

Poetry

Five Modern Poets edited by Barbara Bleiman 0 582 09713 4
Poems from Other Centuries edited by Adrian Tissier 0 582 22595 X
Poems in my Earphone collected by John Agard 0 582 22587 6
Poems One edited by Celeste Flower 0 582 25400 0
Poems Two edited by Paul Jordan & Julia Markus 0 582 25401 9